Horse Sense for Leaders: Building Trust-Based Relationships

Dr. Susan Cain & Debbie Roberts-Loucks

With Foreword by Monty Roberts

Copyright © 2015 by Dr. Susan Cain and Debbie Roberts-Loucks. All rights reserved. No part of this publication may be reproduced, stored in a retrieval system, or transmitted in any form or by any means electronic, mechanical, photocopying, recording or otherwise without the prior permission of the publisher.

ISBN-13: **978-1508480334**

Cover art by Debi Giese, Mode Design Collaborative, modedesignco.com.

DEDICATION

For Monty and Pat Roberts, the dedicated professionals of Join-Up International, and the amazing network of Monty Roberts certified instructors who will bring his message into the future.

ACKNOWLEDGEMENTS

The authors wish to acknowledge the contributions of many who helped bring this book into being: our editors, Taylor Viering and Connie Cain, our publisher, Ben Knerr, and our readers, Tom Loucks, Joyce Dezutti, and Tim and Sarah Buividas, and our Survey Developer, Stephanie Tribo.

CONTENTS

Introduction by the Authors..i

Foreword by Monty Roberts..v

Preparing for a Better Reading Experience:
About Monty's Ground-Breaking, Game-Changing Join-Up® Training..ix

Spotlight on Join-Up:
Interview with Monty Roberts on the Gift of Join-Up..........xi

1. A Transformational Leadership Story: Monty Manages Change, Encounters Resistance, and Overcomes Setbacks in Brazil..1

2. The Four Practices of the Trust-Based Leadership Practices Model..11

3. The Need for Trust-Based Leadership in an Unpredictable World..19

4. Towards a Deeper Definition of Trust......................23

5. The Four Trust-Based Leadership Practices - Be Authentic..33

6. The Four Trust-Based Leadership Practices - Setting Clear Expectations and Consequences......................................43

7. The Four Trust-Based Leadership Practices - Promote Mutual Trust...57

8. The Four Trust-Based Leadership Practices - Expect the Best From Others..79

9. Follow-Up - Ensuring Long-Term Performance Gains....87

10. An Action Plan - Applying Trust-Based Leadership in Your Life and Work...93

11. Take The Trust-Based Leadership Profile...............97

Afterword..107

A Monty Roberts Tutorial..109

About the Authors..111

Additional Resources and Websites...........................113

Other Books by Monty Roberts...................................115

Image Credits...117

Appendix..119

References..129

INTRODUCTION BY THE AUTHORS

We wrote this book to be useful on three fronts: to define and examine the nature of trust, to look at the implications for managing and leading others at work, and to offer specific ways to grow into a more trusting and trustworthy leader. But we are approaching this in a unique way

We are using a live case study featuring a leader who has carved a career as an entrepreneur, who continues to work full-time as a hands-on expert into his late 70's, and who has led one the most massive, largely unpublicized cultural transformations in the history of horse training.

That man is the Horse Whisperer, Monty Roberts, The New York Times bestselling author who has quietly influenced the way that many have come to think of training horses.

Through his first book, *The Man Who Listens to Horses*, Monty launched an international debate about the role that violence plays in training horses. His message has stretched across the globe, but the beginnings of his discoveries date back to his childhood.

Monty is the original Horse Whisperer. He was there before the movie, The Horse Whisperer, was made, before the plethora of current Horse Whisperers crowded the market, even before the Queen of England discovered his work. Once Her Majesty discovered Monty's violence-free horse training philosophy, she made sure the word got out to the rest of the world. *"You must write a book,"* she admonished him when he offered to record his concepts in a video or simple training manual. *"Videos and manuals go away, but a book is forever."*

As hard to believe as this is, Monty has not focused his time on monetizing his concepts and influence as much as he has focused on teaching and applying them to his growing global client network. As refreshing, humble, and honorable as that is, it's not why we chose to focus on Monty as a core case study for this book. The reason we chose him is the inspiration he provides to millions in his mission to end violence and replace it with healing, resolve and trust. And he does it through the most unlikely subject—horses.

Monty Roberts has articulated a strong case for putting trust first in the process of building horse and human relationships. This has become his all-consuming passion; and he works non-stop, 365 days of the year, promoting the cause at home and abroad. New generations have rediscovered his first book, *The Man Who Listens To Horses*, about Monty's successes and failures as he developed his career and became a respected leader.

As the work world advances into a time with the most diverse workforce in history, facing the most complex information age of all time, there exists a core concern: what type of leadership is needed?

One answer can be found by looking at the needs of the next generation of leaders. Young developing leaders are coming into their roles incredibly well-equipped in technical and functional skills. But many of them need an accelerated course in how to manage, influence, partner and collaborate with people.

That's where Monty comes in. He not only offers a real-life example of what a trusting and trustable leader is within his own organization, he teaches trust all over the world.

His primary work is with horses, that's true, but a large part of Monty's impact has been on people. In 2011, Monty traveled to London to receive a special award from Her Majesty, Queen Elizabeth II; he received an acknowledgement for his contributions to ending violence in training practices with horses.

That award was the M.V.O., Member of the Royal Victorian Order, a result of Monty's work on behalf of the Royal Stables. Her Majesty's statements included an acknowledgment of Monty's work globally with people as well as horses. The Queen has been outspoken in her support of his nonviolent message for horses and for people, too. From this point forward, Monty will be known as Monty Roberts,

M.V.O.

This transfer of concepts to humans keeps echoing back from his work with horses. This is what we paid attention to during our study of leadership.

We offer, through Monty's own work and the applicable work of others, a different way to understand the value of trust in the workplace. We hope that you enjoy the stories, and see the value in the themes taken from Monty's equine world.

Dr. Susan Cain,
Debbie Roberts-Loucks
Spring, 2015

FOREWORD BY MONTY ROBERTS

My life's goal is to leave this world a better place than I found it for horses and for people, too. When I first verbalized and began sharing my mission statement, I could not have guessed how many educated and passionate leaders would find the concepts useful in their own pursuits. I did not create these concepts, but only discovered what nature already had in place.

This book exemplifies how leaders of people have extended the effectiveness of the concepts. This has now become one of my primary goals: to assist others to put into practice the important concepts of trust-based leadership.

When I met Clive Warrilow, he was CEO of Volkswagen North America. He brought his leadership team to Flag Is Up Farms and left with the recognition that both of us approached leadership in much the same manner. Like the horse and trainer in the round pen, great leaders give their people room to run.

And not just 'run a little, but run a lot!' When they reach a point where they seek leadership (their flight distance), the leader must be right there. As they seek advice and counsel, leaders invite them to cooperate while seeking help ('Join-Up'). The outcome is that they follow the leader through the trust that has been engendered.

Clearly, *Horse Sense for Leaders* does a great job of illustrating trust-based leadership with the elements I employ when working with horses. Horses can read our intent so I must be authentic and trustworthy if I am to create a willingness within them to learn.

I must set clear expectations and be consistent and fair while we work to achieve the goals. Knowing that horses have no ability to deceive, are only aggressive if we give them a reason to be and only wish to survive, I trust them in return. Creating this partnership allows us to expect the best from one other each day.
Brazil is one of those areas on this earth that desperately needs a reduction in violent behavior. I work with the police who have

created over decades a mentality of 'shoot first and ask questions later.' Abuse of animals is rampant and would seem to be of no concern to most citizens.

The Brazilian pendulum toward violence has swung as far as it can. Many Brazilians now want to move that pendulum back toward the center. At 80 years of age, I will be fortunate if I can start the pendulum, but it is highly likely that moving the pendulum significantly will be left to subsequent generations. The good news is that my early work in Brazil has seemed to find a country that wants a positive change.

The reader should approach this book with an open mind, but I invite being tested on each of my principles. Traveling this globe and sharing the concepts in my 80th year, it's still difficult to predict with certainty what sector of traditional horsemen will change the most dramatically when introduced to Join-Up for the first time. I can assure you that I never expected Brazil, with its centuries of traditionally harsh treatment of horses, to be the fastest to embrace my message of non-violent training.

At the same time that acceptance is being expressed, it is most challenging for me to receive attempts to discredit my intentions or my integrity. I have made it clear for more than 70 years now that my intentions are to reduce or eliminate violence.

My integrity has been 100 percent toward that end throughout my lifetime. I respect, and all leaders should, the need to face hard questions. Every new idea should have to jump through all reasonable hoops to prove its value before being accepted as a plausible answer. The world has chosen to require that I jump through thousands of hoops and my principles have stood the test of time for millions of people and animals.

All who would consider themselves leaders should accept the fact that force and intimidation should be eliminated where shaping the behavior of others is concerned. It is my deep belief that all leaders should cause those whom they affect to accomplish their work because they want to and not because they are forced to. Our globe would be far better off if our world leaders would take on board those principles that the horses have shown us are most important in creating a harmonious existence in the human family, the corporate family or with the animals that experience this journey through life with humans as their partners.

Monty Roberts
January, 2015

PREPARING FOR A BETTER READING EXPERIENCE:
ABOUT MONTY'S GROUND-BREAKING, GAME-CHANGING JOIN-UP® TRAINING

"I don't think anyone ever realizes the power of the message until they see the raw honesty and communication between horse and trainer. It's quite powerful."

- Participant, Night of Inspiration Event at Flag Is Up Farms

What is the topic of this book?

The topic is trust and how it is built using the example of interspecies communication between humans and horses. The book builds on this theme by expanding the understanding of trust via human relationships, particularly between leaders and followers in contemporary

Why is this topic important?

Trust is the primary building block for developing effective relationships at work. Workplaces often unintentionally breed distrust, resulting in disengaged employees and unnecessary, unresolved conflicts. These are the symptoms of trust breaches that are identifiable and repairable.

What can the reader achieve with this book?

This book helps readers connect with the fundamental importance of trust at work, how to lead with trust as a core strength, and what behaviors, skills and tools are readily available to develop a framework of increased trust at work.

The "Trust Conversation" of Join-Up: what is Join-Up, and where can I watch Monty in action?

Join-Up is the foundational training approach that Monty uses to introduce a horse to a human trainer so that mutual trust can develop. Readers will see in chapter seven focusing on The Science Trials that Monty has discovered a faster way to develop trust with horses.

We recommend that you watch a Join-Up here before proceeding:
https://www.youtube.com/watch?v=9Dx91mH2voo

As you watch, ask yourself:

- ✓ How does Monty prepare the environment to encourage trust?
- ✓ How does he encourage trust to develop?
- ✓ How did Monty respond to the horse's reactions?
- ✓ How did Monty's actions allow the horse to choose trust?

SPOTLIGHT ON JOIN-UP:
INTERVIEW WITH MONTY ROBERTS ON THE GIFT OF JOIN-UP

Co-author Debbie Roberts-Loucks interviewed her father, Monty Roberts

Debbie: Can you define Join-Up?

Monty: Join-Up is a process in which a human utilizes a combination of predator and equine signals (typically those of the lead mare in a herd) to propose a relationship of cooperation in which the human will take the decision-makers' position (just as a lead mare in a herd does).

This process is complete when a horse chooses to be with a human rather than away from him. Horses have survived for millions of years, avoiding predators by being ever wary of their environment and only giving their trust to those who have earned it. A horse's first instinct is to take flight from anything they are not familiar with. Imagine the first time a horse meets a human who understands the horse's gestures of communication and "communicates" to him in it.

Debbie: As a teenager, you discovered that horses have a silent communicatic   your lifetime studying and   e in what you call "Equus." Can you tell us more about this?

Monty: These signals are non-verbal, predictable, discernible and effective. The elements are really quite simple, but simplicity becomes their greatest strength.

Debbie: Join-Up is the gift that you developed for the rest of us who needed a process to understand how to communicate with the horse in order to create an environment of cooperation. What prompted you to do this?

Monty: I first developed Join-Up to stop the cycle of violence typically used in traditional horse-breaking. Through a process of clear communication and mutual trust, horses are motivated to be willing partners as they accept the first saddle, bridle and rider of their life in less than thirty minutes.

Debbie: Join-Up evolved into a process based upon communication to create a bond rooted in trust. How does it achieve this?

Monty: It must be nonviolent and can only be accomplished if both partners are relaxed at the end of the process. To gain Join-Up with a horse, it is necessary to step into his world, observe his needs, conditions and the rules that govern his social order. One should learn to communicate in Equus since we know he cannot communicate in our verbal language. This process cannot be faked. Once understood, it is easy to use and can be trust-building for both human and horse.

Debbie: So Join-Up is a tool with which to create a safe and comfortable environment for ongoing communication. Can anyone learn to do this?

Monty: The tool must be used with skill, which may take years to perfect, but in its basic form can be quickly learned. Join-Up works at any stage during this partnership between man and horse, whether it is a new one or one of long standing. Join-Up between human and horse heralds an end to isolation and separation of both our species by bonding through communication.

It is a procedure that should be precisely followed; there are no short cuts. Join-Up may bring out conflict and perceived resistance or even ambivalence. However, if the trainer is competent, believes in the concept and executes it reasonably well, the horse will respond positively. It is imperative that anyone employing Join-Up is totally responsible for their own actions.

Debbie: Since violence must have no part in the process of Join-Up, how can you ensure that the horse will respond the way you hope?

Monty: Violence of any kind will destroy the effectiveness of the procedure. A trainer must move through the process keeping the conversation alive, always allowing the horse time to respond. Join-Up is response-based, not demand-based. The trainer should comply with two significant conceptual rules.

First, time is not the important thing! Good horses are! An equine partner of the highest caliber should be the goal. A trainer should enter the process of Join-Up with the idea that time is not limited. This attitude will maximize results in the minimum amount of time. Horses are animals of synchronicity.

If the trainer's heart rate or adrenaline increases, the horse will sync with this physiology as well. I say, adrenaline up; learning down. Adrenaline down; learning up.

The second most important point to remember is that the trainer waits for the horse to do something right and rewards him. He does not wait for the horse to do something wrong and punish him.

CHAPTER 1
A TRANSFORMATIONAL LEADERSHIP STORY: MONTY MANAGES CHANGE, ENCOUNTERS RESISTANCE, AND OVERCOMES SETBACKS IN BRAZIL

Photo courtesy of Afonso Westphal.

Man in the Arena

"It is not the critic who counts: not the man who points out how the strong man stumbles or where the doer of deeds could have done better. The credit belongs to the man who is actually in the arena, whose face is marred by dust and sweat and blood, who strives valiantly, who errs and comes up short again and again, because there is no effort without error or shortcoming, but who knows the great enthusiasms, the great devotions, who spends himself for a worthy cause; who, at the best, knows, in the end, the triumph of high achievement, and who, at the worst, if he fails, at least he fails while daring greatly, so that his place shall never be with those cold and timid souls who knew neither victory nor defeat."
- Theodore Roosevelt

"I can see people who have been exposed to violence from across the room. That's my demographic."
- Monty Roberts

In Brazil, like much of Latin America, horses are often trained by traditional methods involving force. Training horses in the traditional method involves using an authoritative and forceful leadership style to "break" the horse.

Translated to the work-world, this style recalls the hierarchical, top-down command and control leadership style useful in the manufacturing age, but it does little to engender trust, collaboration, and motivation in today's age of information.

This approach has been replaced by leadership models that engender trust and inspire motivation, styles like charismatic leadership, situational leadership, servant leadership or transformational leadership. The market is crowded with leadership theories, each proclaiming their benefits and respective values.

Transformational leadership is a leadership style where the leader identifies the best possible approach to a situation, and the changes needed to accomplish the vision. The transformational leader then coaches and collaborates with others to execute the changes needed and assure commitment. An effective transformational leaders will wear many hats as they work on transformations.

A good example of transformational leadership – the ability of a leader to inspire followers – can be seen in Monty's Join-Up process, where the horse is transformed from flight animal to trusting partner. There is research to support how transformational leaders impact followers. According to authors Bass and Riggio (2006), there are four components to transformational leadership, what they call the four I's:

1. **Idealized Influence:** leaders are seen as a role model, "walking the talk," and is admired by others who pay attention to what the leaders do.

2. **Inspirational Motivation:** leaders inspire and motivate followers. Their sense of charisma lifts followers to a high performance expectation and to high levels of achievement.

3. **Individualized Consideration:** leaders authentically care

about others, focusing on followers' needs and feelings.

4. **Intellectual Stimulation:** leaders challenge followers toward higher levels of performance, expanding their sense of personal capabilities.

Research shows that transformational leaders are anything but "soft"; groups led by transformational leaders have higher levels of engagement, performance outcomes and motivation than groups led by other types of leaders (Bass and Riggio, 2006).

The key that transformational leadership holds to increasing motivation is the combination of positive expectations and personal challenge. Monty often says, "I don't want my students to be as good as me, I want them to be better than I am."

This exemplifies Monty's transformational leadership approach, inspiring horses and humans to strive beyond complacency, to exceed their normal levels of performance and rise to the occasion because they are encouraged and challenged.

Case Study: Transforming Brazil

Monty has become a transformational leader on a much larger scale with his work in Brazil. Recently, while introducing his concepts there, Monty experienced a setback involving a scam that originated in the country he has helped to transform. Monty was filmed by an unknown saboteur during a horse event where there was a brutal horse-breaking demonstration.

The videographer spliced the film so that it appeared as if Monty was approving of, and possibly even orchestrated, the bloody beating that the demonstration horse endured.

This resulted in outcries from fans across Brazil convinced that they had been duped by Monty's anti-violence message. We will elaborate on this event, but first some background. Prior to this event,

Eduardo Moriera, a prominent Brazilian businessman and successful author, discovered Monty's violence-free methods after undergoing his own setbacks. He wrote a book about his experiences, which became a best seller in Brazil: *Encantadores de Vidas* (A Charmed Life).

He later built the Monty Roberts-Eduardo Moreira Center for Learning to educate others in Brazil about the humane handling of horses. Eduardo commented on the initial impact of introducing Monty's concepts:

"Hundreds of thousands of people have changed the way they deal with horses after Monty's methods were introduced in Brazil. The demonstrations from Monty, the book that I published, and all articles and shows broadcasted in the past months have impacted the country from north to south."

Since that time, Monty has worked diligently to demonstrate the need for a violence-free approach to training young horses through numerous appearances in Brazil. In fact, the Sao Palo Police Academy, Barro Branco, has even embraced Monty's concepts, taken largely from his book, *Horse Sense for People*.

Traditions Give Way to New Thinking

Many in Brazil have chosen to follow Monty's approach and have turned away from the old training traditions of beating horses. These old ways involved teaching the horse to "respect" humans through the use of force. But culture is a strong influence; a need to "prove" themselves to be fearless and powerful still persists among horse handlers in Brazil.

Of course horses, being large and fast, may look imposing, but are actually descendants of much smaller animals that were preyed upon. Horses are flight animals, not fight animals. Monty's methods engage the horse in building trust, much like one would when coaxing a bird or a deer to eat from the hand. Logically, it seems that horses should be "gentled" instead of brutalized during training procedures.

This has been Monty's simple message for decades, one he has repeated throughout the world, transforming people's perspective about horse-training. But changing a long-established culture is a massive undertaking.

On a recent mission to Brazil, Monty emerged from a plane to be whisked away to a demonstration of horse-training hosted by the largest breed association in the country. Once there, he was shocked to learn that the "demonstration" was actually one showing the traditional methods (brutal ways) of breaking a horse.

Monty requested that the demonstration be filmed as an example of the harsh breaking processes still used in many regions around the world. In Brazil, the native language spoken is Portuguese, one that is challenging and unfamiliar in every sense to non-speakers.

Monty's one allocated translator was a young girl named Isabella. As the brutal demonstration began, Isabella left his side to avoid watching the violent show of raw, machismo cowboy action. Now alone and unable to communicate with anyone around him, Monty witnessed the violent demonstration with strangers at his side.

Seeing is Believing

There Monty stood as cameras rolled, pinned in by the crowd and unable to stop the bloody beating that the horse endured. Finally, the horse was led away, and Isabella returned, apologizing for leaving because she could not bear to watch. Monty immediately went to check on the horse, finding him standing in a small, rock-strewn enclosed pen; Monty called in a veterinarian to tend to the battered animal.

After this difficult event, a video was produced and aired on a Brazilian television network. With some creative editing, the traditional demonstration had been spliced with amateur video of pre-demonstration Monty. The video showed Monty looking on, seemingly in approval of the brutalities that the horse was forced to endure. Eduardo gave an accurate picture of the resulting backlash from those who watched the video:

"The initial impact of the current turmoil is clearly negative. I have received many messages from people that say that they no longer believe there are people who care with their heart for animals in this world. They say that they lost their hope. And there is nothing worse than making people lose their hope. It is very sad because I have dedicated a good portion of my life to spreading those concepts and make people believe that there is another way of relating with horses, animals and people using Monty´s methods."

The final result might not be that bad though. Monty always wanted people to know how cruel the traditional way that people started horses throughout the world actually was. Maybe not through the best possible way, but now Brazilians know how cruel it is – and they are shocked. So now they are reacting. As the truth regarding the facts surrounding the setback is beginning to appear, Monty´s image is going back to where it was

People will be willing much more now to adopt a method that does not use violence. Transformational leaders are judged by their actions, and to many in Brazil, this appeared to be an endorsement of the old, brutal ways of training horses. It's an easy call to make, especially when an unknown videographer splices a smiling Monty seemingly endorsing the bloodshed.

In the outpouring of anger that ensued, Monty received death threats and hundreds of angry responses from followers who felt betrayed. To counteract this, Monty and his advisors swiftly opened a civil court case against the perpetrators, and issued numerous reassurances that he would never endorse cruelty or violence.

Transforming Others by Working Through Resistance

Leading change at any level is one of the most challenging tasks of a transformational leader, and Monty is leading from the world stage. "Resistance" is what happens when people encounter change and are unready or unwilling to move through it. Instead, they want to return to comfortable or familiar conditions.

While Monty and Eduardo had made significant progress in Brazil, and people could see the logic and value in their "new" training approach, others clung to the old ways. The video is a perfect example of resistance. Despite the setback of the infamous video, people were awakened to the cruelties of traditional practices.

To further motivate the people of Brazil to change their training methods, Monty did two startling and very effective things. First, he engaged Her Majesty, Queen Elizabeth II, in a conversation about the difficulties and possibilities of transforming the training practices in Brazil with her help. The Queen responded by offering a series of awards for leaders who followed Monty's non-violence approach (Watch the video here http://youtu.be/gauzqQa3yWg).

Secondly, he began holding trainings at his California horse farm, Flag Is Up Farms, focusing especially on Brazilian groups. These were useful beginnings, but resistance is a strong force against change. Understanding Latin culture and expectations helps explain why the resistance to Monty's training methods is so strong.

In Latin cultures, the "culture of honor" is the norm, with expectations that reaching manhood means having the courage to fight. It is also important for men to protect their name, honor and dignity and keep their word. Horse training, then became a natural part of the "proving up" process, and needing to feel powerful and in charge is a great reason to embrace the old ways.

Using force and cruelty to "fight" a seemingly uncontrollable animal, such as a 1200-pound horse, is a potentially convincing way to prove up.

Transforming Others Through Change

Monty, Eduardo, and now the Queen of England were working together to convince millions that training horses involves courage in a different way: protecting the honor and dignity of the horse.

Transforming a culture takes time and consistent support. Through repeated messages, training, and demonstrations, people in Brazil are now learning that horses are flight animals and that their culture of honor can be aligned with the needs of protecting the needs of the horse by using leadership rather than domination.

But this will take the time, patience and the persistence of many world leaders working together. This story illustrates the challenges that leaders have in building trust and inspiring commitment in followers. Most leaders are not building trust on the world stage. They are instead struggling to make sense of relationships at work and in their private lives. To do this, leaders must first learn the language and needs of their constituents. Building trust is far from a one-size-fits-all proposition. In the following interview, Monty discovers the importance of listening to and understanding others at a deeper level.

Interview with Monty Roberts: How Horses Shaped Monty's Values as a Leader

Author Susan Cain met with Monty in summer 2014 to discuss Monty's views.

Susan: Of the horses that you've trained, which ones have the most influence on you as a developing leader?

Monty: Well, Johnny Tivio stands well out in front. Lomitas is a close second. I'm going to say some things that the general public wouldn't understand. I'm going to put third a horse that never had a name; never lived more than four or five years and ended up in a butcher shop.

He's called the "no-name mustang" in my book and he's the horse I was working on in the "Green Corral" in the days when wild mustang races were held.

The Green Corral is where they stored the mustangs that were getting ready for the wild horse races and that's where I got to work in an enclosure. In the wild, all I got to do was observe their natural actions.

In the Green Corral, as I watched the mustangs in the pen, it dawned on me that there was a language; it dawned on me that there was a possibility that a human being could learn that language and could conduct, in some fashion or another, the necessary gestures to cause a horse to respond in what I considered its own language.

The Green Corrals were right next to the rodeo arena in Salinas, California, where I grew up. That's where they fed them and so forth and that's where I where I made my case to Doc Leach, that I could start these mustangs after the race and save some for riding. Anyway, the no-name mustang experience was the first year where I explored the possibility of a language.

I watched him going around this pen and I watched the ear and I watched the licking and the chewing and I watched the lowering of the head and all these things. Mind you, don't give me the credit for knowing that these four things were the gestures at the time that would later become paramount in the language I now call Equus.

I didn't know what the hell I was doing. I had a natural feeling that if I went passive at a certain time, then this horse might respond to me in a favorable way and he did. I remember going to my brother, who was kind of laughing about it, watching the horse following me around. He thought it was funny, a coincidence.

One of the grooms, Wendell Gillott, said, "This is something. You're on to something here. You've got to keep working with this. This is something." He set things up for my first Join-Up, hiding me from my father between the number two and number ten barns in Salinas. Wendell came and he supported me when others did not. My father went nuts when he heard about it and nobody else thought Join-Up had any value whatsoever. Of course, those horses were slaughtered right after the event so my mustang never had a name.

But my brain used that stone in the stream as a touchstone point to trigger me to do everything I've done since that day. So how important was that mustang? Someone might say, "Oh yeah, well another one of those horses would have to do it eventually."

Yeah, what if they didn't and he was the one, so there you are.

CHAPTER 2:
THE FOUR PRACTICES OF THE TRUST-BASED LEADERSHIP PRACTICES MODEL

Photo courtesy of Bob Viering.

"The flight animal only has two goals: to reproduce and survive. And fear is the tool that allows him to survive. This has to be respected in any dealings with a horse, otherwise he is misunderstood.

Man, however, is a fight animal. His preoccupation is with the chase, and having dominion over others in order to eat them or use them for his own ends. So the horse is at the far end of the flight animal spectrum, while mankind is way off the edge of the opposite, the fight animal spectrum. In order to gain a horse's trust and willing co-operation, it is necessary for both parties to be allowed to meet in the middle.

However, it is the responsibility of the man, totally of the man (I'm speaking generically, to include women), to achieve this, and to get to the other side of this hurdle. He can only ever do it by earning the trust of the horse and never abusing its status as a flight animal."
- Monty Roberts

Impacting Others Through Trust-Based Leadership

Monty Roberts holds live demonstrations at his farm throughout the year. Recently, a group arrived in early summer to watch the remarkable transformation of an unstarted horse to accept his first saddle and rider in under 35 minutes. Most traditional horse breaking methods involve days or sometimes weeks of work.

The staff at Monty's Flag Is Up Farms has seen the crowd's reactions many times before: people walking away from the round pen after watching a Join-Up demonstration deep in thought. They witnessed it again as this group dispersed after Monty completed a Join-Up with an un-started horse.

There was disbelief on people's faces and questions on their lips. How, they all asked, could it be that a 1200-pound animal seemingly chose to have a saddle and rider put on its back in such a short time?

The implications of Join-Up took this group, as it does for many others, by surprise. Many cry. Some tear up and want to talk about times in their lives when they experienced force or violence. It is an awakening for many to realize that a horse is a flight animal, a prey animal, despite their imposing size and that violence is not needed to train them. Still others begin to see that violence – as Monty would say – "is always for the violator and never for the victim." All of this comes from a horse, a human and a round pen. The event transforms people.

Leadership and the Importance of Promoting Trust

Karen Stephenson is a corporate anthropologist, author and researcher. Several years ago she proposed her Quantum Theory of Trust. Her premise is that all businesses rely on networks of people within their organizations to drive the knowledge transfer needed to run the company. Her insights have been groundbreaking

Dr. Stephenson's findings have underscored the importance that trust plays in the workplace. Her company has developed software capable of diagramming the buildup and breakdown of "trust networks" or relationships at work. The software generates connective patterns of lines showing how people are linked through information and knowledge sharing. Simply put, it shows the trust patterns across an organization So if trust is the highway that connects people, transformational leaders need to think about the importance of trust, learn to create trust-based relationships and repair the damage that trust breeches cause.

A Trust-Based Leadership Practices Model with Veterans

In the current market-driven economy, it is important to recognize and pay tribute to leaders in the business world who are motivated to high achievement beyond the obvious financial gain. Monty Roberts is this type of leader, relentlessly working in arenas across the world, day and night, month in and month out. People come to hear him for the first time or third or the tenth, to see him start a young horse, or reclaim an abused one, to feel his reassurance that force doesn't work and that trust does.

It's a message spoken with great conviction and gratefully received all over the world. We wanted to connect the dots between Monty's trust-based work, to understand his impact on horses, clients, and colleagues. We wanted to identify the common themes and, hopefully, a working model that Monty uses across disciplines and populations to develop and restore trust.

The most current incarnation of Monty's trust-based model is perhaps the important work Monty is doing to help returning military personnel and first responders in a program called Horse Sense and Healing. In the program, Monty describes working with soldiers suffering from what he calls "post-traumatic stress injury," intentionally replacing the word "disorder" with "injury." The horses do an incredibly efficient job of helping veterans heal, reconnect with a living thing, and regain a sense of mutual trust. Here is another application of Monty's approach that is being used with humans.

Back at Flag Is Up Farms, we interviewed both staff and clients and asked them how Monty's transformational leadership style impacted them. Interestingly, the responses we received strongly correlated to the way that Monty treats horses.

The feedback we received could have been applied to a Join-Up session in the round pen. We found similarities in the way that Monty works, whether with horses or humans. We have gathered the feedback we received on Monty's leadership style into four groups below. We call this the Trust-Based Leadership Practices Model.

Transforming Others Through Trust-Based Leadership Practices

The Trust-Based Leadership Practices Model helps to visualize the leadership behaviors that build trust. Think of a leader whom you have willingly followed. This leader is someone you trust. How would you describe this leader? The Trust-Based Leadership Model exemplifies the traits that allow for the development of human potential through clear expectations and positive expectations.

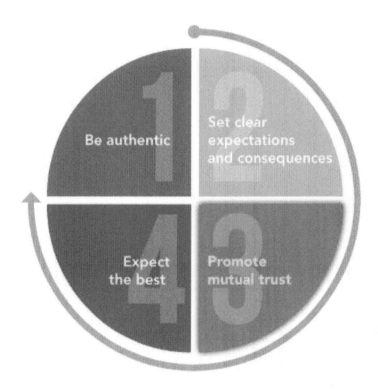

We developed a quadrant model that helps visualize the leadership behaviors that build trust.

1. Be authentic

- Leaders engage others through personal sincerity.
- Leaders reinforce others' sense of individuality and self-worth.

2. Set clear expectations and consequences

- Leaders set clear and fair expectations up front.
- Leaders clarify consequences in an honest and timely way.

3. Promote mutual trust

- Leaders work to eliminate violence and intimidation in their

relationships.
• Leaders act to build and repair trust through open dialogue and inquiry.

4. Expect the best

• Leaders articulate performance goals in compelling and engaging ways.
• Leaders offer meaningful challenges that tap personal motivation.

Together, these four leadership practices make up Monty's unique trust-based leadership model. Common sense should inform all of us that no one model can or should be used exclusively to lead in all situations. Instead, we offer ideas and concepts that have proven to be effective in Monty's practice with horses as well as humans.

In addition to focusing on how others perceive Monty, we offer his own words about the importance of trust. In his "Ask Monty" column, Monty was once asked, "What is more important to training horses: trust or leadership?" and he responded:

"I love this question because it sits at the heart of everything we need to understand before we can be successful in life or with our horses. Leadership is certainly a wonderful quality and, by its very definition, we will find it difficult to rise above mediocrity in the absence of it. Leadership plays an important role in succeeding in our chosen fields, in our relationships with others and as parents if that is a part of our life.

Many important people throughout the centuries would be considered successful because of their leadership qualities. Winston Churchill, Gandhi, and JFK each made their place on the world scene because the masses chose to follow their guidance. So I think by now you would guess that I am going to say that leadership comes first and is more important than trust. Actually, the opposite is true.

One cannot be a leader for his horse or his dog until he first establishes trust with those individuals. As humans, we tend to lie and misinform, creating a form of false trust. It is, however, very hard to lie to a horse or a dog. They can see through us like no human being is able to. Their inherent perception is far greater than that of a human.

TRUST is the most important factor we can generate in our relationship with our horse if we are to be successful in causing him to want to be our partner. Should we choose to BREAK him, we might enjoy the services of a created slave, but we will not get the performance of a willing partner."

- From Ask Monty, by Monty Roberts

Through his vast experience, Monty has distilled the most important leadership factor down to trust, and he has worked relentlessly throughout the world to establish it as the central priority in the training of young horses, and in the rehabilitation of abused horses.

People can't help noticing the alignment between Monty's beliefs and the way he leads his global organization. There seems to be a mix of commitment, dedication, pride, and autonomy at Flag Is Up Farms. Monty as a leader has had a light hand, trusting people who are purpose-driven. This sense of trust is evident in the way things are done at Flag Is Up Farms, and in the regard people have for Monty's work worldwide.

How Trust Impacts Organizational Performance

In his book, *The Speed of Trust*, Stephen M.R. Covey (2006) understood the integral role that trust plays in forming the basis for a successful organization:

"When trust increases, speed increases and cost decreases. When trust is high, customers buy more—more quickly, more confidently, and more often. They stay longer and they refer more of their friends. High trust enables relationships to grow, employee loyalty to soar, stocks to rise, and organizational dividends naturally increase.

When trust is high, the resulting dividend you receive is like a performance multiplier, elevating and improving every dimension of your organization and your life. High trust is like a rising tide, which lifts all boats. In a company, high trust materially improves communication, collaboration, execution, innovation, strategy, engagement, partnering, and relationships with all stakeholders."

The Role of Trust in Monty's Life and Career

If trust forms the basis for a successful business, how did Monty's leadership practices create an international icon, taking him from a railroad car he once shared with his wife, Pat, and three young children, to the gilded riding halls of England?

People are drawn to Monty's books, to Flag Is Up Farms, to the Join-Up process, and to the story of how trust and support trumps violence and force. Many come away with a sense of personal affirmation and renewed courage to tackle the perceived fears in their own lives. It's a phenomenon that many of us at Flag Is Up Farms have seen throughout the years. It's almost as if people who connect with Monty's trust-based message put down a heavy weight, and the relief they feel in expressing their own struggles with violence is palpable

Few leaders have seen their core values expressed across such a global audience. Monty is one of them. People are drawn to stories. Watching Monty place a saddle and rider on a willing and calm horse for the first time in under 35 minutes ignites curiosity in people. Can it be that trust is that important to the process of being an effective leader? If so, they often ask themselves, "How can knowing all this inform my own assumptions about leading others?"

Wonder where you fall on the scale of Trust Based Leadership? Take the survey at the back of the book on Page 117 and find out!

CHAPTER 3:
THE NEED FOR TRUST-BASED LEADERSHIP IN AN UNPREDICTABLE WORLD

Photo courtesy of Afonso Westphal.

"Trust is like air, we notice its importance only when it is polluted or gone."
- **Annette Baier, 1998**

The workplace is one of converging changes: older and younger workers who must rely on each other, people working side by side from vastly different cultures, encroaching competition and the speed of technology that drives urgency to a fever pitch. The Trust-Based Leadership Practices Model can help in this constantly changing environment, offering direction to leaders who struggle with building collaboration, trust, and communication within their organizations.

The Shortage of Trust in Today's Work Environment

According to the annual CEO survey by PricewaterhouseCoopers (PwC) in 2012, 37% of CEOs were worried about a lack of trust in their industry, while in financial services 52% were concerned. These numbers were high enough to cause unease. PwC's results led them to conclude that trust in the world's businesses and leaders have hit an all-time low.

The coming decades will increasingly require a workforce capable of strong collaboration. Baby-boomers will retire or semi-retire in mass numbers. There will be senior leaders turning over control to new leaders. The critical information and knowledge they have will be exchanged and leveraged, or become forgotten and discarded. The coming decades will increasingly require a workforce capable of strong collaboration. According to a labor force projection for 2014 completed by Mitra Toossi of the Bureau of Labor Statistics (2005):

"Baby boomers were between the ages of 40 and 58 years in 2004, and by 2014, they will be in the age group of 50 and 68, which means they went from being a high participation group, to a lower participation group, which causes the overall participation rate to decrease."

Despite baby boomers moving to a lower participation group, they will be retiring at older ages than what has been considered to be the "normal" age of retirement. This is due to the constantly changing and struggling economy; many people today cannot rely on pensions or secure retirement plans. Toossi, (2005), attributes the ability of older members participating in the workforce to "governmental policies and legislation aimed at eliminating mandatory retirement and outlawing age discrimination in the work place."

People will need to think together, create innovative solutions, collaborate to solve problems together and implement solutions together. What is being done to teach collaboration, innovation, and most importantly, trust? Companies will continue to compete on a global scale, with the need to develop trust-based relationships across time, space and cultures.

The answer is that the curriculum has not changed in high schools, technical schools, or even colleges to adapt to these emerging needs. While many business schools offer courses in effective leadership or even in leading globally, they pay only scant lip service to the central need for developing mutual trust in today's workplace.

And of all the human factors that expedite knowledge transfer, innovative leaps, creativity, and collaboration, trust is in the core

DNA of each. Teaching trust is difficult; first, stalwarts who prefer to focus on the task side of leadership have to be convinced that relationships are a critical component of effective leadership. Building relationships is often referred to as developing "soft skills," with the implication that task-focused leadership skills focusing on, technology, accounting and strategy are more important.

In reality, leaders need both soft skills and task-focused skills to function effectively. The workplace, with its abundant diversity, will require leaders who can connect with people across gender, age and cultural differences.

An Interview with Monty Roberts Featuring Two World Leaders: Thoughts on Queen Elizabeth II and Ronald Reagan

Susan: Who have you met that you would consider an example of an effective leader?

Monty: Queen Elizabeth II is so far in the lead in that race, there is just no competition that can equal her. I think she's travelling at 100 miles per hour in the world of being a leader, I think Ronald Reagan travelled at about the same, 100 miles per hour. He had eight years to travel that, and the Queen has had 63.

One of the qualities, in my mind, that makes her that kind of world leader, I hate to say it because it's the thing that bothers me most about her, is humility. She's so humble that she undersells herself, which, to me, takes away from her impact. On the other hand, she says when I ask her about it, "If I didn't have that quality, you wouldn't like me as leader near as much as you do."

Ronald Reagan is another example. He was a really humble guy with an intention for good that very few Americans have ever had. Remember that he stood on both sides of the aisle.

He was a democrat; he was rather liberal for a long time and he moved to a more conservative position when he aged but he never lost sight of the values of the other side of the aisle.

Today, we have many leaders who operate with no integrity whatsoever. We have leaders in the United States that, in my opinion, should be arrested for infractions on the Constitution. Going in and going out, they cannot see across the aisle one inch.

They cannot bear to value the decision of the other side of the aisle because it might cost them when they put their licked finger to the wind. The political breezes do it all now. It's all about expediency and how do I get my popularity up at the moment? Consequently, their popularity soars for very brief times, and then it goes out like a candle because they have not had integrity.

CHAPTER 4:
TOWARDS A DEEPER DEFINITION OF TRUST

Photo courtesy of Bob Viering.

"I was, from a very early age, looking for a way to build a trusting relationship, a 50–50 partnership with a horse. Through my early observation of the mustangs in the desert and being constantly around horses, it occurred to me, as I watched them moving about in a close-knit herd united for survival, that trust and communication were the keys to their success as a species.

After much observation, I could put the rudiments of their language together. I believed that if the horse could trust me, then the whole learning process would speed up. I felt strongly that the answer was through communication. It was many years before I could share my methods with the public."
-Monty Roberts

Defining Trust

The Stanford Encyclopedia of Philosophy provides an interesting definition of trust: "Trust is important, but it is also dangerous. It allows us to form relationships with others and to depend on them for anything. It involves the risk that people we trust will not pull through for us; for, if there were some guarantee that they would pull through, then we would have no need to trust them."

Organizational researchers (Mayer, 1995; Rousseau et al., 1998) define trust this way: "Trust is the willingness to be vulnerable to the actions of another party based on positive expectations regarding the motivation and behavior of the other."

As Monty has shown, communication is vital to build trust in any type of relationship - from horses and humans to co-workers in an office setting.

Trust in the Workplace

Employees face vulnerability every day at work when they do things like float a new idea, take a stand, or try a new approach.

These conditions require the willingness to communicate honestly. Trust directly corresponds to honesty, and employees can tell when their supervisors are not being truthful to them or feel they are being left out of important information and opportunities.

If employees feel they are not getting the deserved respect and are being kept in the dark, it will most likely affect their commitment to the job and their desire to work hard and put forth effort. In the long run, this behavior ultimately impacts the success of the organization. Successful organizations need to make building trust in their organization a priority.

Why Trust Is Needed Now More Than Ever

Author Steven Johnson has suggested that:

"We are often better served by connecting ideas than we are by protecting them... Environments that build walls around good ideas tend to be less innovative in the long run than more open-ended environments. Good ideas may not want to be free, but they want to connect, fuse, recombine... They want to complete each other as much as they want to compete."

The internet has changed the way people work. Consulting group

McKinsey and Associates calls it "the great transformer." People are all driven by the unprecedented speed of information available one mouse-click away.

Steven Johnson is the author of *Where Good Ideas Come From, The Natural History of Innovation*, a book that looks at the macro trends on how innovation evolves. Johnson has studied where good ideas come from and how innovative ideas develop over time.

What he found was that breakthrough innovations usually result from people connecting ideas, or what he calls "slow hunches." According to Johnson, the environments that allow these rich connections are those that are free of the barrier posed by permission-seeking. According to Johnson, "When you don't have to ask for permission, innovation thrives."

Trust is an important component in assuring that innovation can thrive in an organization. The free exchange of ideas moves faster when workers know that positive intent is assumed. In Monty's world at Flag Is Up Farms, different business units, or departments, exist side-by-side. Good ideas come from all of these areas, are informed by access to ideas from outside the organization, and then shared internally by staff to improve processes and functions.

For example, a participant in a training session can introduce a good idea which is then discussed and morphs into valuable changes made. Trust is assumed; everyone knows that the intent of the shared information is to improve.

A Look at Three Emerging Marketplace Changes That Drive the Need for Increased Trust

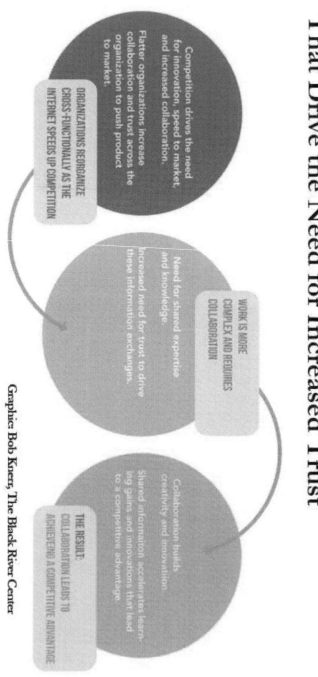

Graphic Bob Knerr, The Black River Center

The Increased Need for Trust in Organizations

Many demands exist that create an increased need for trust in the workplace. The demand for speed to market involves solving complex problems through shared knowledge and expertise. Sharing occurs more often and to a greater degree when trust is present to facilitate learning transfer. An organization's competitive advantage is built on this interconnected network of people who collaborate to create competitive advantage. A more detailed look at this process follows:

1. Organizations Reorganize Cross-functionally as the Internet Speeds Up Competition

A cross-functional organization is an organization whose business model is characterized by interdependent units. Projects flow across functional areas instead of within hierarchical silos in order to increase speed to market and to allow a project access to multiple areas of expert input. In his classic book, *Designing Matrix Organizations That Actually Work; How IBM, Procter & Gamble, and Others Design for Success* (2009), author Dr. Jay Galbraith writes that successful cross-functional, or matrix organizations, are based on personal relationships and trust. The matrix runs on informal communication through personal networks characterized by high trust.

2. Work is More Complex and Requires Collaboration

Companies around the world are experiencing the phenomenon of employee disengagement. Overwhelmed and overworked, many employees become even more despondent when their organizations react by instituting more scorecards and control systems. Companies need a better way to manage complexity.

Morieux suggests simple rules to manage complexity in his book, *Six Simple Rules: How to Manage Complexity without Getting Complicated*

(2014). His rules offer a common-sense look at keeping it simple at work:

- Understand what people do.
- Look for and strengthen cooperation.
- More power to more people.
- Increase interdependence and reciprocity.
- Extend the shadow of the future.
- Reward those who cooperate.

These simple yet profound suggestions form the basis for managing the ambiguity and complexity workers face every day. Notice how these ideas rest on the implicit presence of trust.

3. The Result: Collaboration Leads to Achieving a Competitive Advantage

Innovation is the act of creating something that did not previously exist. Experts state that there are three possible levels of innovation: incremental, semi-radical and radical.

Incremental innovation represents slight changes to an existing product or service. Semi-radical represents a further departure from the existing design, and radical innovation represents a completely new product or service.

Each contributes mightily to helping organizations grow. In fact, to maintain a competitive market position, it will become increasingly more important for every member of an organization to understand and use basic innovation skills, like creative thinking, collaboration and problem-solving. This establishes a creative advantage.

According to the U.S. Council on Competitiveness, innovation will be the single most important factor in determining America's success throughout the 21st century. Interestingly, researchers Bidault and Castello (2010) found that trust is imperative for companies to develop innovation. In their study linking trust to innovation, the researchers found a "sweet spot" in the levels of trust needed for creating innovation. Evidently, too much trust between creative partners can result in a lack of creative tension, resulting in unchallenging and accommodating teamwork behaviors.

The secret, then, is to balance trust with high expectations, as presented in the coming chapter focusing on the leadership practice "Expect the Best."

The Leadership Imperative for Increased Trust

In 1967, author Douglas McGregor defined trust in his book, *The Professional Manager*. "Trust means 'I know that you will not-deliberately or accidentally, consciously or unconsciously-take unfair advantage of me.' It means that I can put my situation at the moment, my status and self-esteem in the group, our relationship, my job, my career, even my life in your hands with complete confidence," (p. 163). Conversely, in his book Trust: A New View of Personal and Organizational Development, Jack R. Gibb describes a fear/distrust cycle that creates low trust in workers. He writes that fear and distrust are most likely to occur when:

- Top management is feared.
- Excessive pressure is placed on people.
- Sales are low.
- Emergencies arise.
- Labor pressures exist.
- The vision of the company is unclear.
- Cultural unrest exists.

Breaking the cycle is critical for organizations to thrive, and understanding how to develop trust plays a key role in doing that.

The Value of Mutual Trust

Engaging employees in important discussions regarding the company and keeping them in the loop on what is happening will increase trust. The bottom line is that leaders and followers must feel that they can trust each other, and when that unwritten contract is broken, they must act to repair it.

Acting to create and repair trust with horses and humans is what Monty Roberts does each day in his busy life. In an extension of his work with horses that was discussed earlier, Monty has developed a program for returning soldiers, called Horse Sense And Healing. His free clinics and workshops have been showcased on the Discovery Channel in documentaries as well as other networks. He cites an important distinction in the repair work he has done with veterans, calling soldiers who suffer from Post-Traumatic Stress Disorder by a new name: Post-Traumatic Stress Injury.

Monty makes a parallel between the trauma and stress that horses suffer and the stress suffered by victims of PTSI:

"Horses who refuse to go into the starting gates at the races have many other similar phobias that trainers deal with on a daily basis. To me, PTSI amounts to the same psychological firestorm that these animals are experiencing. If a psychologist needs his patient to get through a day without killing himself and a dose of some drug will do the trick, then give him the drug; just don't expect it to dramatically change his intention, it simply doesn't work that way."

Every day, people suffer traumas at work, both perceived and real. Leaders must discover and help identify the capacities of their followers to cope and heal. Many workers mask their reaction to stress with artificial exteriors, kill the pain with medications, and never address the root cause. Alienation, fear and trauma can be better managed by restoring trust in relationships and validating worker's individual abilities and self-worth.

Monty has gone on record, stating that:

"Money can be a drug for many people who have never been to war. If family or the government tells us that we're not good enough to make it on our own, we come to believe it. We accept government assistance and, if it is for a sustained period of time, we give up trying on our own. We tend to become like birds in the nest with our mouths open saying, 'feed me.' I work with my warriors to cause an attitude of self-respect and, therefore, the freedom to fend for themselves."

Self-respect and positive self-regard are an important piece, as it turns out, to being an authentic leader. The next chapter looks at the importance of showing up to others in a genuine, authentic way.

CHAPTER 5:
THE FOUR TRUST-BASED LEADERSHIP PRACTICES - BE AUTHENTIC

Photo courtesy of Afonso Westphal.

The Value of Authentic Leadership

- Leaders engage others through personal sincerity.
- Leaders reinforce other's sense of individuality and self-worth.

"It is absolutely amazing that people who have never touched a horse before can accomplish Join-Up. Some of them are trembling with fear and others are doing what they can to show their tough side, acting as though nothing could frighten them. The men and women, large and small, young and old, will act very differently regardless of their size, strength, sex, age or historical background. Not one has ever failed to be visibly moved when the horse chooses to trust them."
-Monty Roberts

There is value when people show up as they really are to others. In their excellent paper, *Discovering Your Authentic Leadership, George*, Sims, McLean and Mayer (2007) noted that, "During the past 50 years, leadership scholars have conducted more than 1,000 studies in an attempt to determine the definitive styles, characteristics, or personality traits of great leaders. None of these studies has produced a clear profile of the ideal leader."

On the other hand, the authors note, "authentic leaders demonstrate a passion for their purpose, practice their values consistently, and lead with their hearts as well as their heads. They establish long-term, meaningful relationships, and have the self-discipline to get meaningful results. They know who they are."

Becoming an Authentic Leader

"Authenticity is a collection of choices that we have to make every day. It's about the choice to show up and be real. The choice to be honest. The choice to let our true selves be seen."
- Brené Brown

According to Dr. Brown:

"Authenticity is the daily practice of letting go of who people think they are supposed to be and embracing who they truly are. Choosing authenticity means cultivating the courage to be imperfect, to set boundaries, and to allow oneself to be vulnerable-exercising the compassion that comes from knowing that people are all made of strength and struggle. Nurturing connection and a sense of belonging can only happen when people believe that they are enough."

Just as Monty wrote books reviewing his life's journey, the first step to becoming an authentic leader is to review one's life and to become more "self-aware," as leadership experts suggest. Self-awareness often comes from difficult experiences.

The authors George, Sims, McLean, and Mayer (2007) found that the 125 leaders they interviewed reported that motivation came from difficult experiences. The authors report that, "The leaders reframed these events to rise above their challenges and to discover their passion to lead.

Leveraging Life's Challenges: A Case Study From Monty's Life

Sometimes it is easier to avoid making a statement, standing up for a belief, or taking a stand. Monty was put to the test in this case study from the book *The Man Who Listens to Horses* The case study illustrates the real impact that core beliefs can make and the courage it takes to believe in oneself:

"I received a phone call that would change my life. Queen Elizabeth II of England had heard about my methods. She invited me to England to give a demonstration. Once I arrived and had successfully demonstrated a Join-Up, some expressed disbelief remained.

I would learn that the Queen had spoken with her staff and they'd suggested to her that I had done something underhanded with the horses when I was supposedly taking them through the ring to acclimatize them – in short, they suspected some form of trickery.

The Queen hadn't agreed with their judgment, but, nonetheless, she'd asked what they would need to see in order to be convinced that my work wasn't fraudulent.

They'd suggested that a truck be sent over to Hampton Court to pick up two very large, three-year-old piebald stallions, who were very raw and had barely been handled; they'd certainly never seen me or the round pen. They proposed to take them one at a time off the truck and see if I could start them – predicting I would fail.

The Queens's equerry, Sir John, told me he wanted me to start these horses without acclimatizing them to the ring. Because my working methods were new to him, I suppose it didn't seem like much of a request. However, it's unfair to expect horses to go through an experience that must rank as the most traumatic of their lives and be introduced to a frightening new environment at the same time.

This new plan concerned me, as there was enough pressure on the event already. I was in a fish-bowl. It was important that everything went well, and naturally I wanted the right measures taken to give me the best chance.

.There were 100 guests invited to see the demonstration that afternoon, as well as the stable staff who were now lining up against the wall – and I knew they were expecting me to fail so my work would be judged as false.

Sir John took the microphone and stepped into the round pen to introduce me. The huge piebald colt came charging towards him and slapped his big front feet on the ground, exhibiting anger over the whole situation.

So, Sir John stepped quickly back outside the gate and made the introduction from the other side of the fence, and you couldn't blame him.

I was not happy about these new circumstances, which I felt were unfair as well as dangerous. This big colt was aggressive and, in addition, continually distracted by his friend's calling from just outside the building.

Suddenly, everyone stood up – the Queen had walked in. She wasn't scheduled to be here, but she had turned up to see the outcome of this. She went to an area behind where the seats were located and gestured to everyone that they might sit down.

Sir John continued with his introductory speech and explained what they were about to see. I couldn't do much else but step through the gate into the round pen, pick up my line and give it a go."

Monty did indeed succeed in joining-up with the huge colt. The Queen was so impressed that she thereupon decided to adopt Monty's training methods.

The Value of Drawing From Real Life Experiences

Authentic leaders draw their inspiration from their own life experiences. Monty has made it a life mission to *"leave the world a better place for horses, and for people too."* He has developed a career path based on his early experience of abuse from his father. Monty took his early experiences and personal truths and did an interesting thing; he redirected his repulsion, anger, and sadness and went in the opposite direction by training horses with a trust-based approach instead of a fear-based approach.

At first, his ideas were not popular or well-understood by others. As a child, one way Monty escaped from his father's brutality was by watching herds of wild horses. He learned first-hand that horses, like deer, are "flight animals," not "fight animals."

He watched as mares used gestures in their own silent language to school youngsters in the herd. He adapted this language to work with the gestures of a predator that horses understand, and he now uses every day in his training. He calls the language of the horse "Equus," and his discovery (that trust-based communication is a more effective way to train horses) is now widely accepted and endorsed.

At first ridiculed for thinking that violence had no place in starting young horses, Monty has now built an empire on his core thinking. People could call Monty's discovery a "disruptive innovation," an idea that forever changes the status quo in an industry. His ideas were endorsed by a handful of "early adapters" who saw value in his work. But the critical mass of mid- and late-adapters did not embrace his ideas until later in his career. Now his ideas have become mainstream, endorsed by industry leaders and the Queen of England.

But Monty took the first lonely steps, creating a radical departure from mainstream horse training. Monty's core beliefs infuse his work with purpose and sustainable growth. He did not abandon his beliefs, even under great pressure. He built an empire based on what he knows to be true.

Leading the empire requires a certain entrepreneurial spirit as well as the self-worth needed to sustain momentum.

Steps To Becoming a More Authentic Leader

"Owning our story and loving ourselves through that process is the bravest thing that we will ever do." - **Brene Brown**

The graphic below illustrates the steps a leader can take to become actively authentic, to own and practice who they really are. The questions help to think more deeply about drawing from your real-life experiences:

Checklist: Finding Your Unique Abilities

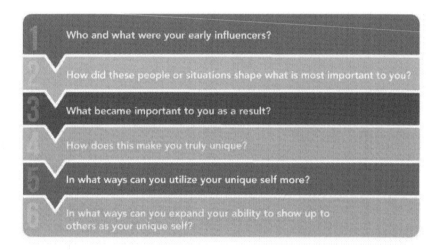

Together, these questions form a reflective approach to thinking through the process of becoming an authentic leader.

Attributes of an Authentic Leader

Researchers have found that authentic leaders hold certain attributes (Dirks & Ferrin, 2002 and Mayer et al. 1995), found that for trust to grow, the trustee (i.e., a leader) must possess three characteristics that are critical for the development of trust:

1. Ability
2. Benevolence
3. Integrity

According to Avolio, Gardner, Walumbwa, Luthans, and May (2004), *"authentic leaders build benevolence and integrity with their followers by encouraging open communication, engaging their followers, sharing critical information, and sharing their perceptions and feelings about the people with whom they work; the result is a realistic social relationship arising from followers' heightened levels of personal and social identification."*

Work by Jung and Avolio (2000) suggests that leaders may build trust by demonstrating individualized concern and respect from followers. It is also known from social exchange theory (Blau, 1964) that a realistic social relationship is likely to lead to gestures of goodwill being reciprocated, even to the extent of each side willingly going above and beyond the call of duty (Konovsky & Pugh, 1994).

Recapping the First Practice: Be Authentic

Circling back to the first practice, Being Authentic, we have found through feedback from interviews with Monty and his staff that two practices support the ability of a leader to be authentic:

1. Leaders engage others through personal sincerity. Leaders who show up as themselves, with imperfections and humility, come across as more sincere and credible.

2. Leaders reinforce other's sense of individuality and self-worth.

Leaders demonstrate their ability to go beyond judging to acceptance, respecting, appreciating and valuing others.

This chapter has considered the definition of an authentic leader, the value that authentic leaderships offer, and steps to becoming a more authentic leader. In Monty's words, "leading authentically is the only option, because the horse is the final judge."

Interview with W. Andreas Jacobs

W. Andreas Jacobs is Executive Chairman of Jacobs Holding AG, Executive Chairman of Callebaut AG, and Vice-Chairman of Adecco SA. Dr. Jacobs is internationally recognized and respected in the horseracing world. He has worked with Monty numerous times; perhaps most famously with his legendary race horse Lomitas.

As a leader yourself, how do you see Monty's impact in the world?

Dr. Jacobs: Monty's key impact is on how the world is dealing with horses. Since he has demonstrated his methods, the world has changed. Horse people understand that there are peaceful and painless ways to start and train a horse. This is a huge change for millions of horses. Especially because Monty is sharing his methods with the world, he is teaching students and riders through courses or videos, allowing his methods to spread around the globe.

But his classes where he applies his methods to a human-to-human scenario are equally breathtaking, covering all ages and all social standards. I have seen him talking to well-known corporations, who rated his "take-home-value" the highest.

What do you feel are the most important leadership qualities?

Dr. Jacobs: The ability to motivate a group of people in the organization by being human, touchable, emotional, all based on solid values and a well prepared and communicated strategy is the most important leadership quality. To motivate people, you have to show them the next level; how exciting and enriching it can be with progress and achievements. I was given the chance to quadruple the size of our chocolate business between 2003 and 2013.

The share price today is eight times what it was in 2003. And we became the largest cocoa and chocolate manufacturer, producer of about 25 % of the world's cocoa, and 20% of the world's chocolate. This was solely a team effort. We were steering the team, based on solid values and a thoroughly developed strategy.

What do you feel Monty's most important leadership attributes are?

Dr. Jacobs: Monty is a very generous leader. He is constantly sharing his insights and teaching others to observe and learn. He created a large learning center, trying to leave something behind for the next generation to build on, to make the world a better place.

CHAPTER 6:
THE FOUR TRUST-BASED LEADERSHIP PRACTICES - SETTING CLEAR EXPECTATIONS AND CONSEQUENCES

Photo courtesy of Afonso Westphal.

The Value of Setting Clear Expectations and Consequences

• Leaders set clear expectations upfront.
• Leaders clarify consequences in an honest and timely way.

"Join-Up is the process of communicating with the horse to create an environment of cooperation. I will fully explore all of the elements of this procedure. I intend to break down the essential elements of Join-Up to educate you not only of its

importance, but how to do it. The reader should fully understand that the execution of the principles of Join-Up is likely to produce a partnership with the horse, virtually eliminating the creation of remedial problems.

It is important for all horsemen to know that remedial problems are, in almost every instance, the product of training error. If I were to write the perfect book and every reader did a perfect job of executing the principles, there would be no need to discuss recommended procedures for dealing with remedial problems. It is a given that I will not write the perfect book and no reader will understandably work without mistakes. With that knowledge in mind, I will include on these pages practices that I have discovered to be effective in dealing with man-made problems.

Since the horse is a flight animal, he reacts and responds rather than initiates. This fact dictates that the presence of what we perceive as a remedial problem is caused by us and our shortcomings. If the horseman conducts his training each day with these facts clearly understood, it is likely that he will reduce the potential for creating negative behavior."

- Monty Roberts, from his textbook *From My Hands to Yours: Lessons from a Lifetime of Training Championship Horses*

Leaders Set Clear Expectations Upfront

It is interesting that much of Monty's work with horses is remedial, correcting the behaviors that horses receive and interpret from their human counterparts. This also goes on far too often in the workplace, where there may be a lack of clear expectations or an absence of expectations to follow. The job of many leaders is not only to express their expectations clearly, but to conduct remedial and repair work with those who have received no expectations or unclear or inaccurate expectations.

A Closer Look at Setting Clear Expectations

It has been said that complexity is the silent killer of business. If that is the case, then today is an age where information flows so freely that the "faucet" is turned on all the way, 24 hours a day. Communication scholars refer to this as "noise in the system," and it is a force that leaders have to negotiate themselves before they can help others through. People have gone from a world of static messaging to a multi-dimensional communication landscape, and there is no going back.

Many savvy leaders know that good ideas can come from anywhere in an organization. Innovation and creativity are suddenly everyone's business. Leaders can inspire followers to see through the complexity, grapple with possibilities, share feedback, and act on expectations? Business consultant and author Ron Ashkenas' book, *Simply Effective: How to Cut Through Complexity in Your Organization and Get Things Done*, contains some very useful advice for setting clear expectations. He has created a useful list of avoiding the wrong things to do when making requests of others.

The Seven Deadly Sins of Making Demands

1. Backing away from tough expectations: Framing the expectation or goal as a choice, so it can become easily ignored or minimized.

2. Engaging in charades: Knowing that this is a "fake work" initiative; there is no real hope of accomplishing the task.

3. Accepting see-saw trades: When employees take on one goal, they are relieved of another one.

4. Setting vague or distant goals: There is no detailed time frame, clear definition, or the goal is set too far into the future, so no one takes it seriously.

5. Not establishing consequences: There is no differentiation between those who successfully achieve goals and those who do not.

6. Setting too many goals: Setting too many objectives allows others to prioritize goals according to preference, instead of importance.

7. Allowing deflection to preparations, studies, and research: People are allowed to spend time planning instead of committing to a real goal.

Setting expectations clearly is a critical step in establishing mutual trust. It's important to determine these "deadly sins" when thinking about communicating expectations to others.

Setting Clear Expectations – A Round Pen Case Study

Monty is clear in his notions of a response-based setting (instead of a demand-based setting) to help horse and humans increase mutual trust:

"Join-Up is a tool, like a fine chisel, with which to carve a safe and comfortable environment for ongoing communication. The tool must be used with skill, which may take years to perfect, but in its basic form can be quickly learned. Join-Up works at any stage during this partnership between man and horse, whether it is a new one or one of long standing. Join-Up between you and your horse heralds an end to isolation and separation of both our species by bonding through communication. It is a procedure that should be precisely followed; there are no short cuts. Join-Up may bring out conflict and perceived resistance or even ambivalence.

However, if the trainer is competent, believes in the concept and executes it reasonably well, the horse will respond positively. It is imperative that anyone employing Join-Up is totally responsible for their own actions. Violence must have no part in the process of Join-Up. Violence of any kind will destroy the effectiveness of the procedure.

A trainer must move through the process keeping the conversation alive, always allowing the horse time to respond. Join-Up is response-based, not demand-based. The trainer should comply with these two significant, conceptual rules."

To set the clear initial expectation that a horse can choose to join him or not, Monty emphasizes this:

"I say don't go away a little, go away a lot. Consider your options. Come and Join-Up with me and I will protect you, or stay out there on your own. But you can trust me. There is an environment near to me and it is perfectly safe."

The Join-Up Guide to Trust-Based Leadership

Setting clear expectations upfront with others prevents a lot of misunderstandings and assumption-building later on. When Monty enters a round pen to work with a horse he has never seen before, he uses a stylistic approach that builds mutual trust. First, he speaks the horse's language, a language of gestures Monty has named "Equus."

He sets the first expectation clearly, he makes a gesture for the horse to "go away." Then, instead of a demand or a sharp whip, Monty stands ready to support the horse when s/he is ready to "Join-Up," putting an end to the horse's sense of isolation and fear.

The most effective leaders know that putting an end to isolation and fear at work involves communicating effectively. Leaders have available to them a mesmerizing array of web-based communication options from which to choose. Most leaders embrace technology to enhance their communication reach, but problems can arise when leaders replace in-person conversations with more impersonal approaches.

Using the same incremental learning process created by Monty in the round pen, we have recreated the Join-Up conversation for human use.

Monty's Join-Up Conversation Guide

In the round pen, Monty Roberts starts horses by introducing them to a trust-based approach. The round pen almost acts as an accelerator, allowing trust to develop as a foundation in the relationship. A similar process can be applied to conversations at work and outside of work. The Join-Up conversation is a trust-building conversation that can be used to clarify and share information or redirect another person.

1. **Set expectations for a positive learning experience.**

2. **Build a conversation that explores individual perspectives and encourages honesty and sharing.**

3. **Join-Up: Identify common goals**

4. **Follow-Up to assure commitment to action**

1 Ask to meet and name the reason. Share your positive intentions:

2 At the meeting, work through this conversational framework. Remember to remain relaxed:

Explain why the meeting was called. Thank the person for coming.

Describe the issue needing discussion, new expectations or changes needed, and why they are important to discuss.

Use "I" not "we" statements.

Name your emotion about the situation.

Express your desire to ensure that the issue is resolved or needed changes occur.

Turn the conversation over and listen actively.

Talk through resistance or ambivalence with respect— name the resistance you see with respect and clarify for understanding.

Manage the "emotional load" by naming emotions instead of expressing them.

Recap and restate concerns, aims, and goals expressed from both sides.

3 Join-Up by identifying the mutual goals that you both share:

Check to ensure that both choose the mutual goals and agree on them.

Brainstorm optional ways to achieve the goals.

4 Follow-Up by sharing clear next steps and expectations for needed actions

Many say that setting clear expectations is a matter of showing instead of telling, in order to help others decide, as Monty does. Showing others why an expectation is important sometimes involves telling compelling stories, keeping the message simple, and allowing the story to create urgency. Mark Twain once said, "Don't say the old lady screamed. Bring her on and let her scream."

Expressing clear expectations can help others get a sense of urgency, a clear need and how the expectation can meet that need.

Holding Others Accountable: The PIC-NIC Feedback Model

Monty discovered a useful adaptation of a B.F. Skinner model for setting and holding consequences he learned from psychologist Dr. William Miller. In his *Ask Monty* column, Monty offered a detailed explanation of the model and how to use it with horses:

Question: How much time do you have after your horse has made a mistake to effectively correct it?

Monty: Most of the top behaviorists of the world will agree that where horses are concerned we have about three seconds after the action in order to effectively reward or discipline. One should remember that human nature suggests that we are much more apt to discipline immediately than we are apt to reward immediately. Since reward is every bit as important as discipline, we will tend to fall far short in that category The term P.I.C.N.I.C. is often used to label a rule which governs this phenomenon. P.I.C. stands for Positive Instant Consequences and N.I.C. stands for Negative Instant Consequences. The key word is Instant, recognizing that we have three seconds in which to express contentment or discontent with the actions involved.

If your horse seems to be a slow learner or continues to cause you trouble over a sustained period of time, one might take a hard look at the timing you accomplish in the area of the PICs and NICs. Bad behavior is almost always our fault and not the fault of the horse.

Human leaders can benefit from this concept by offering consequences in the form of consistent feedback. Studies show that younger employees first entering the workforce want feedback often. Feedback is critical to building performance in followers.

Giving Effective Feedback: The Key to Employee Accountability and Engagement

Most employees think about feedback in terms of their once-a-year review or the time they got the riot-act read to them by their boss when they messed up last year. For a significant amount of employees, the idea of getting feedback is both stressful and angering. It isn't their fault.

Only two percent of managers and leaders are trained how to effectively communicate with employees (Stone & Heen, 2013) which leaves a lot of room for mistakes, especially when it comes to giving feedback. The existence of this gap is surprising as there is a great deal of research that shows the advantages of giving effective feedback and conversely, the costs of not giving enough feedback or giving bad feedback.

For most employees, the biggest (or worse, only) source of feedback they get is their annual performance review. This is problematic as four out of five employees are unsatisfied with the quality of these reviews (Batz, 2013).

Employees feel that that these reviews are not an accurate account of their performance and rarely give them specific ways that they can improve. Studies show that these employees are about two times as likely to seek new employment versus those who see their reviews as accurate (Jacobsen, 2013).

Another concern that employees have with feedback is that they view it as mostly negative. Some employees feel that the only time their managers notice them is when they mess up. Leaders need to address this problem, as 67% of employees are motivated to work harder when they are praised by their leader. (Jacobsen, 2012).

Praise for good performance is an important facet of effective feedback and has massive effects on employee satisfaction, engagement, and performance (Thorne, 2013). This isn't to say that negative or critical feedback shouldn't be given to employees as critical feedback is an important part of improving performance and coaching; but employees need praise and encouragement from their managers as well.

The final major gap in feedback for employees is the actual delivery of feedback. As mentioned above, only 2% of managers are trained how to communicate with employees (Stone & Heen, 2013). This leaves a lot of room for bad communication practices, especially when it comes to giving feedback. Poorly delivered feedback can, at best, lead to no or little changes in employee behavior or performance, or, at worst, lead to disengaged and unhappy employees (Thorne, 2013).

With the largest feedback gaps identified as frequency, content, and delivery; the important question is how to address and fix them. For frequency, the obvious solution is simply to provide more feedback. In the business world, this is often easier said than done. Priority projects, important meetings, and pressing deadlines will always swallow up time for a leader. To counter this, leaders need to put feedback as its own priority.

Tips for Improving Feedback

First, schedule time on the calendar for giving feedback. Spend five or ten minutes here or there writing emails praising good work. Set up coaching feedback meetings after seeing coworkers turn in projects and deliver presentations. Remember, a majority of employees would like to receive feedback or praise weekly (Jacobsen, 2013). Secondly, use two different approaches: positive feedback and negative, or redirecting feedback.

Positive Feedback

Use praise for reinforcing performance and individual coaching sessions for improving poor performance. For praise to be effective, it should be genuine and detailed. Employees can easily tell if a manager is giving them insincere or false praise. False feedback is ineffective as it can discourage and frustrate employees.

To prevent this, tell employees specifically what they did well or why you as a leader appreciate them. Simply telling employees, "Great job" doesn't tell them much, but highlighting their specific contributions and strengths will make them feel valued and drive engagement (Kaput, 2013). Strive to give employees positive feedback that is genuine, detailed, and when acceptable, public. Some employees prefer private feedback, so leaders should ask each person how they prefer positive feedback.

Negative Feedback

Giving negative feedback, sometimes called redirecting feedback, is one of the most important skills a leader can have. Giving negative, or redirecting feedback effectively is much different from delivering praise. To start, negative feedback should be delivered one-on-one, in a private meeting. Critical comments given in front of an employee's peers can lead to that employee feeling angry and frustrated at their leader or company (Kaput, 2013).

Negative feedback should be direct and focused on improving performance opportunities. Researchers have found that it is useful to describe the specific undesirable behavior; don't make generalizations or assumptions (Stone & Heen, 2013). For example, telling an employee that "rolling your eyes when someone is talking can be seen by others as unprofessional" is preferable to "you've got to fix that bad attitude."

Finally, be respectful and empathetic. Negative feedback is hard to hear and uncomfortable. Understanding this and learning to deliver negative feedback in a calm, respectful manner will go a long way in making sure given feedback is received and acted upon.

Recapping the Second Practice: Set Clear Expectations and Consequences

Effective leaders know that trust grows when followers can depend on clear expectations and consequences. Take a look at the two actions that support setting clear expectations and consequences:

1. Leaders set clear expectations upfront.

As hard as it can be to boldly set expectations, effective leaders know that expectations mobilize people to action. Setting expectations early in the process of a project keeps performance on course.

2. Leaders clarify consequences in an honest and timely way.

Teachers know that consequences teach, and that good teachers only facilitate the exchange. People learn by experiencing a consequence for their actions, and adapt their behavior accordingly. Effective leaders help followers connect with consequence so followers can choose the outcomes they prefer.

To illustrate how Monty leads, Adam Bates from Flag Is Up Farms was interviewed.

Interview with Flag Is Up Farms Employee Adam Bates

Question: What type of leadership attracted you to work with Monty?

Adam Bates: Monty provides his expectation and allows you to succeed or fail. This provides the framework for adding additional skill sets in an environment that rewards positive outcomes, but understands that some individuals may not have a certain skill set.

Unlike many employers who helicopter over the menial human mistakes ("you forgot to turn off the light"), Monty looks at the big picture and sees if you are helping create a better place for horses and humans, or hindering that process. Monty understands that adrenaline drives anxiety up, and that this will cause learning to go down.

CHAPTER 7:
THE FOUR TRUST-BASED LEADERSHIP PRACTICES - PROMOTE MUTUAL TRUST

Photo courtesy of Bob Viering.

The Value of Promoting Mutual Trust

• Leaders work to eliminate violence and intimidation in their relationships.
• Leaders act to build and repair trust through open dialogue and inquiry. Leaders act to build and repair trust through open dialogue and inquiry.

"As a child I watched my father apply the principle, 'You do what I tell you to, or I'll hurt you!' to the horses that went through his hands. He often applied the same concept to me. Did the horses feel the same resentment that I did toward the needless pain inflicted upon them? I do not recall learning anything through being physically punished except how to avoid such an incident.

Even then, I questioned whether an environment dominated by pain, and therefore fear, was productive. I obeyed him because that was what my father wanted. I loved my horses and knew that I wanted good relationships with them, surmising that there might be a better way.

I was, therefore, from a very early age looking for a way to build a trusting relationship, a 50–50 partnership. Through my observation of the mustangs in the desert and being constantly around horses, it occurred to me, as I watched them moving about in a close-knit herd united for survival, that trust and communication were the keys to their success as a species.

After much observation, I could put the rudiments of their language together. I believed that if the horse could trust me, then the whole learning process would speed up. I felt strongly that the answer was through communication. It was many years before I could share my methods with the public. I produced good horses and no one knew how. After my father died, I went public. The rest is history."

- Monty Roberts from *The Man Who Listens to Horses*

Research Supports the Efficiency of Mutual Trust

Research supports the effectiveness of Monty's trust-based methods. Recently, a quantitative scientific study was completed comparing the traditional approach to starting a horse with Monty's Join-Up approach. The results are startling.

Case Study: The Science Trials

The study was completed by Dr. Veronica Fowler, Dr. David Marlin, and Dr. Mark Kennedy, and was carried out at Sparsholt College in the United Kingdom in the summer of 2009, and accepted for publishing August 30, 2011 in Anthrozoös, a quarterly, peer-reviewed multidisciplinary journal reporting the interactions of people and animals.

A selection of 14 untrained horses were utilized in the study. Two methods were compared:

1. The UK conventional style of training (CT), and
2. The Monty Roberts technique (MRT).

The results turned out to be surprising. Four mares and ten geldings between the ages of three and five were sourced from a variety of non-competition yards in the UK.

To ensure that each trainer had an equal proportion of horses with similar temperaments, horses were matched based on the level of difficulty when being lead in hand as well as behavioral reactivity to a novel object test (the sudden opening of an umbrella).

The matching (pairing) of the horses was then tested using a statistical test (Mann-Whitney U test) which confirmed that there was no statistical difference between the paired horses. Following this, one horse from each pair was randomly assigned either MRT or CT.

Trainers were selected in order to represent two differing styles of training horses. Monty Roberts (MRT) represented his own techniques. Phil Roelich, an accomplished and experienced conventional British Horse Society registered trainer of 12 years, represented the conventional technique (CT).

Each trainer requested material and was permitted one assistant trainer, and each trainer was allowed 30 minutes per day to work with each horse for 20 days. Following this, the horses undertook a standardized ridden obstacle test. Heart rate monitors were used during the daily training sessions and the final assessments were recorded using a Polar RS800CX system (Polar Electro, Finland).

The training session included a standardized ridden test filmed by a team of dedicated camera operators. Finally, a panel of judges, who were "blinded" from knowing which trainer they were comparing, viewed video footage of each session and scored the results of the training impact and progress made. The study was approved by an independent Ethics Committee at Sparsholt College (Hampshire, UK) prior to being undertaken.

In the first week of the study, (days 1-7) all of the Monty Roberts (MRT) horses had experienced Join-Up on at least four separate occasions, saddled, bridled, long-lined and ridden freely inside and outside of the round pen. All completed the ridden obstacle and ridden flatwork test and had also been introduced to training sessions.

In comparison, all of the conventional training (CT) horses had been saddled, bridled and lunged, however no horse had yet to have been ridden for the first time. Components of the ridden obstacle and ridden flatwork test had not yet been introduced to training sessions.

During the late phase of training (days 8-20), all of the MRT horses were being ridden freely around the arena. All components of the ridden obstacle and ridden flatwork test were now being included in the MRT training sessions and being ridden as per the test.

In comparison, all but one (ridden for the first time on day nine) of the CT horses were being ridden freely around the arena. Components of the ridden obstacle and ridden flatwork test had also now been introduced to training sessions. Despite these clear differences in rate of training progression, there was no significant difference between MRT and CT trained horses in minimum, mean or maximum heart rates throughout 20 days of training.

A Score Card: Understanding the Advantages of the Trust-Based Approach

All MRT horses were saddled and ridden on day 1. In comparison six CT horses were saddled on day 2 and the remaining horse on day 3. CT horses were ridden on day 4 (three horses), 5 (two horses) and the remaining two horses on days 7 and 9.

During first saddle and rider, MRT trained horse had significantly lower maximum heart rates (bpm) when compared to CT, and lower average heart rates (bpm) when compared to CT.
CT horses' average heart rates were increased at the time of the first saddle and first rider in comparison to heart rates observed during 20 days of training. MRT horse's average heart rates were equivalent, or less than, at the time of their first saddle and first rider (respectively in comparison to heart rates observed during 20 days of training).

During the first saddle and rider, the MRT trained horse had significantly lower maximum heart rates (bpm) when compared to the CT horses. CT horses average heart rates were increased at the time of first saddle and first rider in comparison to heart rates observed during 20 days of training.

MRT horses average heart rates were equivalent or less than at time of first saddle and first rider respectively in comparison to heart rates observed during 20 days of training. The MRT approach for initial training of riding horses appears to be more effective than the CT approach as determined by significantly lower maximum heart rates during the first saddle and first rider, and significantly higher performance scores during standardized ridden tests following 20 days of training.

A SCIENTIFIC COMPARISON OF HORSE TRAINING METHODS

THE COMPARISON: Monty Roberts Training vs. Conventional Training

THE TEST: Training horses for 30 minutes a day for 20 days

THE METHOD: Trainers got 7 horse that were monitored for heart rate and training progress

THE RESULTS: Training Progress...

MONTY ROBERTS TRAINING			CONVENTIONAL TRAINING		
	Saddled	Ridden		Saddled	Ridden
Horse 1:	Day 1	Day 1	Horse 1:	Day 2	Day 4
Horse 2:	Day 1	Day 1	Horse 2:	Day 2	Day 4
Horse 3:	Day 1	Day 1	Horse 3:	Day 2	Day 4
Horse 4:	Day 1	Day 1	Horse 4:	Day 2	Day 5
Horse 5:	Day 1	Day 1	Horse 5:	Day 2	Day 5
Horse 6:	Day 1	Day 1	Horse 6:	Day 2	Day 7
Horse 7:	Day 1	Day 1	Horse 7:	Day 3	Day 9

THE RESULTS: Heart Rates...

AT FIRST SADDLE: Monty trained horses had significantly LOWER heart rates compared to conventionally trained horses

AT FIRST RIDE: Conventional trained horses had much HIGHER heart rates than Monty trained horses

THE OVERALL: Monty Roberts trained horses TRAINED FASTER and had LOWER HEART RATES than conventionally trained horses!

Looking closely at the Science Trial results, it is clear that something is causing the Monty Roberts trained horses to progress faster and farther in a shorter period of time than their conventionally trained counterparts. That causal factor is the research variable known as Join-Up. By emphasizing relationship first, instead of performance demand first, a strong interdependent network of trust has been forged between horse and human.

How Mutual Trust Builds Networks in Organizations

Dr. Karen Stephenson, as mentioned in Chapter Two, analyzes trust networks in organizations. What she has found is that trust serves as a kind of information highway between people. She calls her theory *The Quantum Theory of Trust* (Stephenson, 2005). She believes that trust is the force that holds together networks of people. Her ability to quantify that trust is a critical ingredient to organizational success is what distinguishes her from other social researchers.

Dr. Stephenson (2005) has found that organizational effectiveness and innovation, and the development of new ideas, all rest on the power of social networks that exist in organizations. According to Stephenson, people all live in a "galaxy" of social networks. People identify others to trust and to go to for particular types of queries or needs. This network drives perceptions and influences the decisions that people make. If that is the case, consider the relatively small number of people that leaders rely on to make tough decisions.

Why Mutual Trust is Difficult to Grow in Organizations

In his blog, *The Uncanny Valley of a Functional Organization*, Ben Thompson (2013) talks about why vulnerability and mutual trust are such hard things to manage in organizations:

"Collaboration is one of those buzzwords that will get you wasted in a drinking game; it's on the lips of every innovation consultant, thought leader, and CEO.

HORSE SENSE FOR LEADERS: BUILDING TRUST-BASED RELATIONSHIPS

The concept – working together to make something great – seems straightforward, but the fact is, it's the proposed cause that is hard to achieve."

It is easier to understand the reason why when you understand what goes into true collaboration: mutual trust and respect, and the willingness and freedom to disagree.

Both ingredients are really hard for humans in groups. Start with mutual trust and respect: we're all naturally suspicious of those we aren't intimate with, and that's compounded by the anxiety of status and salary inherent in a workplace. It's even worse at top companies, where nearly every employee grew up the smartest kid in their class and can't help but try to prove they're still the best.

As for disagreement, it's actually the willingness that is more challenging than the freedom. It turns out we humans usually want other people to like us. In fact, we usually want other people to like us more than we want to make something great, so we hesitate to criticize and point out flaws.

As critical as mutual trust is within an organization, it is hard to embed in organizational cultures. Increasing mutual trust in an organization may involve practicing the following conditions:

1. Mutual respect
2. Willingness and freedom to disagree
3. Demand for honesty at the expense of being liked

These three conditions form a foundation for trust to develop and for innovation to thrive. When the famous Aeron chair was being developed at Herman Miller, designers Bill Stumpf and Don Chadwick led a talented team.

As they worked to create the most well-known ergonomic office chair ever made, the team created breakthroughs in design and material use. The chair became the first to replace upholstery with the breathable, form-fitting Pellicle suspension that adapts to virtually every body. The team embodied the three principles and then some.

They became available to each other day and night. The mutual trust they shared allowed the team to develop, revise and implement an iterative learning approach together. The development of trust came before product design and delivery.

In his book, *Why Relationships First Works*, author Joe Camp (2011) commented on the importance of starting horses with a solid relationship prior to training:

"We were lucky enough to stumble onto Monty Roberts' Join-Up before our first horse ever arrived, and that's where we began with each one of our new herd. Then we discovered Join-Up… and it made such an absolute difference for us to establish relationship first and true leadership right from the get-go. Our herd members are now all willing partners who never stop trying. It very simply changed everything with our horses."

Building Trust One Brick at a Time: The DNA of Mutual Trust

Many people think of trust as an emotion. But trust is a capacity; the capacity of one person to let go of control and turn it over to another. Famous outdoor challenge pioneer Robert Knerr (1987) wrote about how to strengthen the capacity of trust; he likened it to stretching a rubber band. According to Knerr:

"First, in order for trust to occur, an individual must willingly turn over control to another person. This engages the capacity of risk-taking, and a sense of vulnerability is the result. By giving up guarantees and taking a risk, a person then needs to ask for help and support. This engages the capacity of acceptance, the capacity that allows us to fulfill our needs. This in turn creates a sense of dependability between both parties. This sense of dependability is a self-perpetuating, self-reinforcing process. I ask for help, I let go, I receive help, I accept help. This is a process that benefits the giver and the receiver, bonding them in a mutually-trusting relationship.

Now, in order for capacity like trust to grow, all off these capacities must be in some way touched- letting go of control, asking for help and accepting help.

Through repetition, these capacities are expanded and other counter-productive capacities (like mistrust) are contracted, until trust is accepted and even chosen. It can become self-perpetuating."

Graphic: Bob Knerr, The Black River Center

Knerr's Mutual Trust-Building Model

The model illustrates how mutual trust is built and becomes self-reinforcing, or as Knerr writes, self-perpetuating. It is important to look at how mutual trust can be intentionally developed.

Consider Monty Roberts in the Round Pen. In Join-Up, the conditions are created for the formation of mutual trust to develop. Trust is then accelerated, in a kind of time-lapse sequential order. Monty can achieve the initial steps of getting a horse's first saddle, bridle, and rider on in under 35 minutes. This is the power of mutual trust.

Below is an empirical perspective of the Join-Up process. The process of Join-Up suggests that certain conditions can accelerate the development of mutual trust.

The Join-Up Conversation Guide for People: Strengthening Motivation to Change

We have extrapolated from the Join-Up process the conversation that takes place between humans and horses to include a conversational framework between a leader and a follower. The conversation offers a means to stimulate real change, with a primary focus on respect and the welfare of the other person.

Leaders are tasked daily with a need to resolve issues, introduce a change or clarify an expectation. This guide will assist in getting through the conversation with the intent of building mutual trust and accelerating motivation to change. This framework is informed by empirical observations, interviews with a variety of observers, and comparisons to other problem solving conversation models.

The Join-Up Conversation Guide

Graphic: Join-Up Conversation Overview

1. Set expectations for a positive learning experience.

2. Build a conversation that explores individual perspectives and encourages honesty and sharing.

3. Join-Up: Identify common goals

4. Follow-up to assure commitment to action

A Detailed Look at How to Hold a Join-Up Conversation

This conversation allows trust to develop quickly, much like it does in an enclosed round pen. This conversation should be held privately, and in a setting that reduces tension and allows for full focus on the conversation.

The goal of the Join-Up Conversation is to construct a clarifying conversation rooted in trust that can produce lasting results for both parties. The conversation helps both people think together about the best way forward. It can also be adapted to use as a performance building conversation, as a problem solving conversation, as a coaching or feedback conversation and as a conflict resolution conversation.

1. Set expectations for a positive experience:

Start the conversation by letting the other person know that you would like to meet, and name the issue or concern. Make certain that your intentions are perceived as helpful instead of threatening.

Key Comments (These have been created as suggestions only):

- Ensure that you communicate positive intent.
- Suggested comment: "I value your contribution, and would like to set some time aside to talk about (name the issue)."
- If the other is not open to meeting, leave the door open by

emphasizing positive expectations and intentions and suggesting that when he/she is ready, you will be available.
- If this is not an option and an immediate change is needed, directly set a time and place to meet. Reassure the other of your positive intentions.

2. At the meeting work through this conversational framework. Remember to remain relaxed (adrenalin down, learning up):

Adjust your tone and tempo to mimic the other person's while introducing the topic and focus of the conversation. Reassure the other person of your intentions to develop a two-way conversation. Set three ground rules for the meeting: mutual respect for opinions and thoughts, mutual fairness and mutual honesty.

Key Comments:

- Thank the other for coming and name the issue again.
- Suggest three ground rules: "I would suggest that we both agree to mutual respect for each other's ideas, fairness to the other person, and personal honesty as we see things."
- Use "I" instead of "We" statements.
- Express your desire to ensure that the issue is resolved or that the needed changes occur.
- Turn the conversation over to the other person and listen actively; accept silence and show patience.
- Talk through resistance or ambivalence with respect—objectively name the resistance you see and ask for the clarification needed to understand. Manage the "emotional load" by naming the emotions you feeling instead of expressing it.
- Recap and restate concerns, aims, and goals expressed.

3. Join-Up by identifying the mutual goals that you both share:

Check to ensure that both choose the mutual goals and agree on them. Brainstorm optional ways to achieve the goals.

Key Comments:

- Name the mutual goal(s) to be achieved. Name the benefits of the goal(s).
- Ask, "How can we get there?"
- Ask, "How ready am I/are you to commit to this (these) goal(s)?"
- Ask, "What do I need from you and what do you need from me to commit?"
- Work to resolve ambivalence by discussing any remaining role or goal ambiguities.

4. Follow-Up by sharing clear next steps and expectations for needed actions:

Create a short and simple plan to achieve the goal(s). Discuss any additional support needed, the expectations of each person, and agree on a strategy and/or timeline to check back on progress or problems that may occur.

Key Comments:

- Agree on the changes and next steps needed to achieve goals.
- Create a short and simple plan to achieve the goals, including responsibilities of each person.
- Discuss any additional support needed.
- Agree to check back on progress or problems.

Case Study:
Monty Roberts on Creating Trust in the Round Pen

"In the environment of the round pen, I can set up response-based communication. The configuration of the round pen allows the horse to flee, yet remain at the same distance from me. If the pen is oval or rectangular, the horse could simply go to the point furthest from me. This would tend to break up the flow of motion and make smooth communication more difficult. The flight distance of the horse is the distance he is apt to use trying to maintain a safe distance from his pursuer.

This usually amounts to about a quarter to three-eighths of a mile. Once flight is no longer his choice, the horse will instinctively begin to communicate with his pursuer, tending to circle. Nature has instilled the understanding that if the horse continues to flee, he is likely to encounter another predator, eventually lacking the energy to successfully escape. Through ¬survival of the fittest, the horse has come to ¬realize that he is more likely to survive by conserving energy through communication and negotiation.

The creation of willingness within your horse is possible only in an environment free of fear and resentment. To create a place free of these two elements, you must eliminate violence and force as an option and establish parameters of cooperation using discipline that is acceptable and bilaterally agreeable. I have concluded that the best way to do this is to establish a system of contracts.

With people, you can have verbal contracts or written contracts. With horses, your contracts must take place with actions speaking as loudly as the spoken or written word. The effective equestrian will create these contracts so that when lived by, a path of least resistance is set up. This path is then designed so that the horse willingly takes you to the goals you want for him.

We know that in many circumstances a horse comes into this environment with distrust, fear and/or anxiety. Through communication in a language the horse understands, we can create change to allay these phobias. It is important to increase the workload if the response you get is not the one you want.

This effectively creates a contract, and one which the horse is apt to willingly consider. A response is the first step toward change and it is change that we are seeking. Any response should be viewed as a portal through which you can pass to create positive consequences and thus begin the process of negotiation."

From Monty's perception, fear has no place in the learning process, and it's absence allows trust to accelerate the willingness to learn and change. The following interview with Dr. William Miller provides insight into the process of human *motivational interviewing*.

The Power of Join-Up: How a Similar Trust-Based Approach has Helped Humans

An Interview with Dr. William R. Miller

William R. Miller, Ph.D., is Emeritus Distinguished Professor of Psychology and Psychiatry at the University of New Mexico. He co-founded motivational interviewing with Dr. Stephen Rollnick. Dr. Miller has been recognized as one of the world's most highly-cited scientists by the Institute for Scientific Information.

Dr. Miller's primary interest is in the area of the psychology of change, but his research and practice spans the treatment of addictive behavior, self-regulation, behavior therapies, spirituality and psychology, motivation for change, and pastoral psychology.

Like Monty Roberts, Dr. Miller has made a profound impact in his chosen field. He has changed how clinicians think about the nature and treatment of substance use disorders. Like Monty's Join-Up method, motivational interviewing avoids creating resistance and denial by employing an active and empathic approach. Find out more at www.williamrmiller.net

About Motivational Interviewing

Motivational Interviewing (MI) is a collaborative, person-centered form of guiding to elicit and strengthen motivation for change. It is designed to fortify an individual's motivation for (and movement toward) a specific goal by eliciting and exploring the person's own arguments for change.

The spirit of MI is based on three key elements: collaboration, evoking or drawing out, and autonomy. Research indicates a clear correlation between client statements about change and outcomes. In other words, the more someone talks about change, the more likely he/she is to change.

As a Professional Development Coach, MI is used to elicit change and development from coaches by giving them a sense of autonomy and control over their own circumstances. MI is most effective when used within a developed coach-coachee relationship.

1. Can you tell us how Motivational Interviewing is like Join-Up?

Well to start with, the very term "Join-Up" implies a collaborative partnership. It is not one person ordering and coercing, but two people working together with mutual respect. Each one has important expertise. Most often motivational interviewing has been used in helping relationships to facilitate change.

It is not about trying to install something (like motivation) that the person lacks, but rather bringing out that which the person already has. There is deep listening involved, paying careful attention to this particular person, accepting where he or she is without judgment, and together finding how to move ahead. I see Monty giving that kind of careful respectful attention, in the moment, to whatever a horse is telling him. It helps to bring out the best in those with whom you work.

2. How did you first encounter Monty and his work?

The first time I saw Monty working was on a BBC film on public television. I sat down transfixed, and what struck me was that "He's using the same kind of approach that I do in counseling, but he's doing it with HORSES!"

I sent Monty our demonstration videos of motivational interviewing, and when we finally met for the first time he said, "I didn't need to take notes. You do the same thing I do, but you're doing it with ALCOHOLICS!" We were equally fascinated.

3. What do you feel Monty's most important leadership qualities are?

As a teacher/trainer he has taken the time to specify exactly how to work with horses - what you actually do, not just abstract ideas. He can describe it, show it, and teach it to others. I find that he teaches in the same way that he practices – by coming alongside with a gentle conversation, never getting too far ahead of the person's readiness to hear and understand.

4. As a leader yourself, how do you see Monty impacting the world?

He's a man on a mission of non-violence. Besides transforming the world of horse training to make it more humane, he also attracts people who recognize something in his methods that can apply in human relations as well.

In the addiction treatment field, professionals used to talk about "breaking down" patients, very similar authoritarian language that justified highly confrontational humiliating treatment that would be regarded as malpractice in almost any other area of mental health care. I use a Join-up video in my own training because it communicates the same collaborative spirit of motivational interviewing in a powerful, visual, nonverbal way.

So many of Monty's aphorisms also apply in human relations!! If you act like you're in a hurry and only have a few minutes, change may take all day if it happens at all. If you have a relaxed and uncluttered mind and act as if you have all day, you may see amazing change in a matter of minutes.

5. How can leaders use key MI concepts as a framework for facilitating change?

So much of leadership is in how you think about your role. As you move upward in a management pyramid, does it mean that you get to boss around more and more people, or that you are serving an ever larger number of people?? If you tell yourself, "I have to make these people change," it becomes a power struggle.

If you assume instead that those you work with have underutilized talents and creativity that need to be tapped, often enjoy their work, and are capable of self-direction, you are likely to take a more collaborative approach. Each is a self-fulfilling prophecy.

Recapping the Third Leadership Practice: Promote Mutual Trust: Leaders work to eliminate violence and intimidation in their relationships.

1. People work in result-driven environments that cause leaders to seek ways to expedite work. Leaders can help followers accomplish expectations without force by thinking about the suggestions from this chapter.

2. Leaders act to build and repair trust through open dialogue and inquiry.

3. Trust breaches happen for many different reasons. Leaders can help repair mistrust by considering the suggestions in this chapter.

This chapter has reviewed the critical function of building and repairing trust. Through detailed examination, the anatomy of trust has been reviewed, and a how-to guide offered for a Join-Up conversation.

CHAPTER 8:
THE FOUR TRUST-BASED LEADERSHIP PRACTICES -
EXPECT THE BEST FROM OTHERS

Photo courtesy of Bob Viering.

The Value of Expecting the Best From Others

• Leaders articulate performance goals in compelling and engaging ways.
• Leaders offer meaningful challenges that tap personal motivation.

The Case for High Expectations and the Link to Performance

Expecting the best from others may seem at first to be a naïve but well-intended leadership practice. But study after study verifies the link between high expectations and follower performances.

For example, Lumsden (1997) found that a characteristic shared by highly effective teachers is their adherence to uniformly high expectations. They refuse to alter their attitudes or expectations for their student, regardless of the students' race or ethnicity, life experiences and interest, and family wealth or stability.

Brophy (1986) advises teachers to "routinely project attitudes, beliefs, expectations, and attributions...that imply that your students share your own enthusiasm for learning. To the extent that you treat your students as if they already are eager learners, they will be more likely to become eager learners."

The Pygmalion Effect: Livingston's Work

In the workplace, the phenomenon of followers responding to high expectations is called the Pygmalion Effect. The author J. Sterling Livingston was on the faculty of the Harvard Business School from 1941 to 1971. He wrote a Harvard Business Review Classic article that was originally published in 1969.

In his article, *Pygmalion in Management*, Livingston used George Bernard Shaw's play, Pygmalion to illustrate the potentially transformative impact that leader/managers have on followers. Livingston noted the difficulty that leaders/managers have in creating positive expectations for followers. He offers several suggestions based on his own work; focus on follower's first year because that's when expectations are set, match new hires with outstanding supervisors, and set high expectations for yourself as manager/leader.

Effective leaders, then, create high performance expectations. These formative findings were followed by decades of leadership research that has spanned three ages of economic evolution- from the industrial age, to the information age and into the conceptual age. In his book, *A Culture of Improvement: Technology and the Western Millennium* (2007) Robert Friedel observed that,

"Technology and the pursuit of improvement are ultimate expressions of freedom; of the capacity of humans to reject the limitations of their past and their experience, to transcend the boundaries of their biological capacities and their

social traditions."

So transformational leaders who expect great things from followers give them the freedom to experiment, "push-back" and achieve. In an article in The Economist *entitled* The Age of Mass Innovation *(2007) authors Vaitheeswar and Carson cited an interesting quote by Tim Brown, CEO and President of IDEO, an International design and consulting firm founded in Palo Alto, California; "Creative people like to challenge constraints and authority."*

And William Weldon, chairman of Johnson & Johnson, the health-care giant, observed that: "Innovation is no longer about money, it's about the climate: are individuals allowed to flourish and take risks?"

The Demand for a New Set of Expectations: Daniel Pink on the Conceptual Age

In his book *A Whole New Mind,* author Daniel Pink explains how the economy has evolved and is now moving toward what he calls the conceptual age. According to Pink, the conceptual age is a swing toward a time of globalization, abundance, outsourcing and automation.

Businesses are now more dependent on the tools that drive business and not produce goods. For example, there is a greater need for creative thinking, product design, collaboration and meaning-making.

Virtually every area of industry will now require leaders and managers who can, in effect, raise performance levels and create the innovative climate needed to reengineer competitive ability in their organization.

This relates to a useful illustration of Join-Up and Monty Roberts. Consider the horse in the round pen. The horse is met with an inescapable challenge; join with a leader who can transform his fear, identify with that leader enough to follow him, and learn to adapt and change in the innovative climate called a round pen.

Case Study: Transforming People in India

Dear Mr. Roberts,

It was a great experience to see you in action in Delhi. We hope to see the videos so please share the link. My daughters Ameera and Ayesha will enjoy this new style of training, which fits well with how they view horses and indeed show respect for all animals.

Kind regards,
Amir, Delhi Training Attendee

The Brooke (www.theebrookee.org) is an 80 year old leading international animal welfare charity. They work in partnership with local people in the poorest parts of the world, across Africa, Asia and Latin America to ensure that working horses, donkeys, mules, and their owners live a better life.

In September 2014, Monty traveled to India by invitation of the Brooke, to see the impact of the charity's equine welfare work.

Monty wanted to go to India to promote a non-violent approach toward horse handling and to advance his mission to leave the world a better place than he found it, for horses and for people, too.

Monty spent a week visiting rural communities around India to see the positive impact the Brooke is having on working horses and donkeys. He visited the Brooke's District Equine Welfare Units in Sonipat, Muzzaffarnagar and Baghpat – all within a few hours of Delhi. There, Monty met local service providers, Brooke staff, and the communities who are directly benefiting from the Brooke's work, and made the following comment:

'I have been looking forward to seeing the Brooke's work for myself since first hearing about this wonderful charity years ago. Through my own program and mission statement, I hope to improve the lives of horses and humans alike and the Brooke's fundamental aim is the same. This will be my first time in India and I

am excited to meet with local communities, see how the Brooke staff engage with them, and provide useful tips along the way to help improve the lives of these hardworking animals and their owners."

Petra Ingram, the Brooke's Chief Executive, accompanied Monty on the visit. She commented that, "We're very excited to finally show Monty the important work that the Brooke does all over the world. We share a core belief with Monty that all animals have the right to a life free from violence. Horse lovers around the world admire and respect Monty's gentle approach towards horse handling. This is something we at the Brooke encourage in our day-to-day work with communities. To have someone of Monty's stature so dedicated to seeing our work first-hand is extremely encouraging and proves we are having a huge impact. We look forward to introducing him to our work in India, and hope it will be the first of many field visits."

Monty also visited the Beri Equine Fair where animals are bought and sold and where the Brooke had a mobile clinic providing veterinary treatment and advice to owners.

The Brooke works in 11 different countries across Africa, Asia, the Middle East, and Latin America, and in 2014 celebrated 80 years of helping improve the lives of working horses, donkeys, and mules.

Brooke field staff conducts regular assessments to identify and monitor equine welfare conditions. The data collected indicates which welfare issues are affecting different groups of equine animals, and allows them to create effective projects to address them.

Motivating Others with High Expectations: Leaders articulate performance goals in compelling and engaging ways.

In his book, *Drive, The Surprising Truth about What Motivates Us*, author Dan Pink discusses the importance of keeping work interesting and rewarding. Pink asserts that long-lasting personal motivation comes from three sources: autonomy, mastery, and purpose. Together, these three motivators drive individuals to perform at their best. Pink shares a story about the Atlasian Company, where employees are given an opportunity to work on projects that interested them, on company time.

The result was a spike in innovation and product development, and in turn, revenue. Given the opportunity, most of us will seek personal challenges that have meaning to us, allowing us to work toward our own mastery.

Making work meaningful is perhaps the most important challenge of transformational leadership. In his monograph, *An evaluation of conceptual weaknesses in transformational and charismatic leadership theories*, Gary Yuki (1999) suggests that leaders use these actions to articulate compelling performance goals:

- Develop a challenging and attractive vision, together with employees.
- Tie the vision to a strategy for its achievement.
- Develop the vision, specify and translate it to actions.
- Express confidence, decisiveness, and optimism about the vision and its implementation.
- Realize the vision through small planned steps and small successes in the path for its full implementation.

As Monty demonstrates, transformational leaders motivate followers with a compelling business vision and provide their followers with the autonomy they need to master complex tasks. Passion and purpose are consistently demonstrated in the leader's actions. And as we have seen, with the right conditions, personal motivation can be ignited within any of us.

Recapping the Fourth Practice: Expect the Best from Others

This chapter has examined how leaders can ignite motivation in followers by clearly articulating performance challenges, helping followers through the change process and holding accountability for action.

- Leaders articulate performance goals in compelling and engaging ways
- Leaders who create urgency to action engage followers in understanding goals and their vital role in reaching them.
- Leaders offer meaningful challenges that tap personal motivation.

Everyone seeks meaning in their life and work. Personal motivation is switched on when people meet a meaningful challenge that requires effort and the promise of learning and feeling personal achievement. This chapter has reviewed the essential need to "raise the bar" and expect the best from others.

CHAPTER 9:
FOLLOW-UP - ENSURING LONG-TERM PERFORMANCE GAINS

Photo courtesy of Bob Viering.

"What your relationship turns into after Join-Up depends upon you and how good a leader you are."
- Joe Camp, author, writer, producer, director, author, passionate speaker, and the man behind the canine superstar, *Benji*

The Steps to Effective Follow-Up: Communicating Clear Next Steps and Expectations

Follow-up is a critical step in assuring that expectations are implemented. Here are some steps that leaders and followers can negotiate to ensure success:

• Agree on the changes and next steps needed to achieve goals.
• Create a short and simple plan to achieve the goals.
• Discuss any additional support needed.
• Agree to check back on progress or problems.

Follow-Up in the Round Pen

In the round pen, trust is earned after completing a Join-Up. Monty builds on this essential trust bridge by turning away from the horse and inviting him to follow. Next, he places the first saddle and bridle that the horse has ever encountered on to the horses' back. As a leader, Monty continues to show positive intent and remain non-confrontational. The horse trusts Monty and is willing to take a risk. The saddle is new for the horse; he needs some time to get used to accepting a different kind of challenge.

Monty shows empathy by allowing the horse time to get comfortable. Monty remains calm even during the stressful change process, and gives the horse the space he needs to adapt.

Steps to Creating an Effective Follow-Up Process

Below are the steps needed to complete the Follow-Up phase in a useful Join-Up Conversation.

1. Agree on the changes and next steps needed to achieve goals

In the round pen, Monty introduces a new, but clear expectation; a new goal to accomplish.

- **Leadership tip:** As a leader, make sure that the mutual expectation is clear. To get rid of assumptions, ask the other to recap what they know about the goal. Invite questions.

2. Create a short and simple plan to achieve the goal

Follow-Up is a two-way trust conversation; Monty accepts the horse's reaction, and helps him work through the change process to assume his new role.
- **Leadership tip:** A good plan has no more than three objectives, within a prioritized list.

3. Discuss any additional support needed

While Monty shows empathy, he raises the bar of accountability. Instead of lowering his expectations, Monty supports the horse to reach the performance levels needed.

- **Leadership tip:** Lead by offering choices instead of using force.

4. Agree to check back on progress or problems

The feeling of mutual safety that Monty has created allows additional goals to be accomplished. In the case of the round pen, it is the horse's first rider.

- **Leadership tip**: Create a realistic timeline to allow check-in's on progress, not just the targeted result.

As a leader, anticipate that setbacks are part of the learning process. Encourage on-going communication, by agreeing to check back on progress or problems.

Setting Clear Expectations

Setting clear expectations and next steps is a key part of becoming a trust-based leader. Learning to set clear expectations involves being specific and detailed, listening and answering questions, staying with the conversation through conflicts, and setting consequences when necessary. In the article *How The Best Leaders Build Trust* Stephen M.R. Covey wrote:

"Consider the example of Warren Buffett -- CEO of Berkshire Hathaway (and generally considered one of the most trusted leaders in the world) -- who completed a major acquisition of McLane Distribution (a $23 billion company) from Wal-Mart. As public companies, both Berkshire Hathaway and Wal-Mart are subject to all kinds of market and regulatory scrutiny. Typically, a merger of this size would take several months to complete and cost several million dollars to pay for accountants, auditors, and attorneys to verify and validate all kinds of information. But in this instance, because both parties operated with high trust, the deal was made with one two-hour meeting and a handshake. In less than a month, it was completed. High trust, high speed, low cost."

Interview with Joe Camp, Author of The Soul of a Horse and creator of the Benji series

What strikes you as the most profound impact that Monty has made as a leader?

Joe Camp: We humans are in such a hurry that there's no time to build a relationship, to learn to communicate, to gain and give understanding. Why do I feel so strongly about Monty Roberts' Join-Up? Because it answers the why questions right up front.

Why does it work?

Joe Camp: Because it speaks to the horse's genetics in the horse's own language, the language of the herd. Which is all built upon the fact that the horse is a prey animal, a flight animal. And safety and security are his number one concern, at the top of his forever wish list. The horse would always rather be in a safe and secure relationship than not. And most importantly...anyone can do it! Join-Up is simple. Easy to accomplish. Straight to the point, using a very specific "1-2-3" kind of "to-do" list that anyone can understand and handle. I managed to accomplish Join-Up after watching Monty's DVD only twice.

Why does it cause the horse to – as you say – change forever?

Joe Camp: Because the horse does the joining-up of his own free will. He chooses you, not vice-versa. It's his choice whether or not to say to you I trust you to be my leader. If you in any way coerce the horse into being close to you, into accepting you or your training, there will be no change in the horse. The willingness, the "try" will not be there.

What your relationship turns into after Join-Up depends upon you and how good a leader you are. In other words, how well and how easily you can move the horse's every-body-part whenever and wherever you want. Another concept that is sometimes hard for humans to grasp: the simple idea that who moves who can determine leadership, bolster relationship, and select one's place in the herd.

Is Monty's Join-Up in a round pen the only way to begin a relationship with your horse?

Joe Camp: No, of course not. There are more ways to Join-Up than one can count. Our Mouse had not been exposed to the round pen Join-Up when she made her choice to Join-Up. It all happened with Monty in a "square pen". In Iowa it took six men to get Mouse into a trailer to come to Monty. It took Monty ten minutes to convince her, using her language, to come to him and say I trust you to be my leader. A moment later Monty was addressing his group of students using Mouse's back as a podium to lean on. Just amazing.

CHAPTER 10:
AN ACTION PLAN -
APPLYING TRUST-BASED LEADERSHIP IN YOUR LIFE AND WORK

Photo courtesy of Bob Viering

Some of the concepts in this book may be more useful than others, and apply to different areas of your life. The central concepts are presented below:

• Replace fear in the workplace with a constructive learning environment characterized by clear expectations, freedom of choice, and support for learning from setbacks and failure.

• Seek to understand followers and their fears, motivation and expectations.

• Surround followers with an on-going conversation about the challenges they face, how the challenges impact them and how everyone can work together to overcome them.

- Stretch the imagination and ignite the motivation of followers by clarifying compelling goals and anticipating that they can reach them.

A Personal Action Plan

Think about mapping out a few ideas to enhance your impact as a leader:

1. Describe the ideal leadership style you would like to consistently practice.

2. In order to do that, name several things you could start working on.

3. What will you need to do more of?

4. What will you need to do less of?

5. What will you need to continue to do that you are doing well?

Applying Trust-Based Leadership Practices in Your Life: An Interview with Business Leader George Isaac

George Isaac is the Founder and President of GAI Capital Ltd. and its George Isaac Consulting division, a fifteen year-old investments and management consulting firm.

Isaac has over 30 years of management consulting and business leadership experience in both privately held and public companies. He has served on numerous public and private corporate boards. After a distinguished career as a Deloitte Consulting Partner, CEO and EVP, Isaac started his own consulting firm focusing on family business issues centered around leadership, performance improvement, family dynamics, governance, and succession. Isaac is a frequent speaker at national and international conferences and has several published articles available at www.GeorgeIsaac.com.

How did you first encounter Monty and his work?

George Issac: Around 10 years ago through a Young Presidents' Organization education meeting where Monty presented his leadership principles learned from working with horses to our organization of business presidents. We also visited Monty and Pat at their home several times, most recently in 2014 for further learning and exposure to his horsemanship.

What do you feel Monty's most important leadership qualities are?

George Issac: As leaders, we must first listen and seek to understand, and then take action. Monty at a young age understood these key leadership skills that take many of us years to figure out. His mastered the art of skillful communication, careful listening, and thoughtful understanding that helps to relate to animals, and are the same skills that produce the most effective leaders. His ability to relate to horses through trust and communication provides living proof that these techniques are the best roadmap for successful leadership, appropriate for most organizations

As a leader yourself, how do you see Monty impacting the world?

George Issac: Monty's teachings on non-violence through improved communication, listening, and understanding would help alleviate much of the turmoil, distrust, and destruction taking place around the globe. We are fortunate that Monty has taken his Join-Up lessons on horse gentling to leadership and relationship management training. His message needs to get out to more country heads of state, politicians, and business leaders. I am thankful we have Monty as a mentor for current and future leaders.

Anything else?

George Issac: On a more personal note, I volunteered with no recent riding experience to participate on my first ever three-day cattle drive. I studied Monty's book on relating to horses and used that as my training for handling my horse. As a result, I bonded wonderfully with my horse using Monty's non-violent, trust-based riding style.

It was particularly meaningful when one of my rough and tough buddies with spurs thought I was too soft on my horse. He wanted to teach my horse who was boss and asked to ride him. After an initial hard spurring, the horse took off and galloped away. My friend immediately lost control of the horse and never got it back—all in front of us brand new cowboys!

I immediately took the horse back from my cussing friend, went to my horse's nose and hugged him and apologized for the prior "tough-guy" rider. I got on, made a soft clicking noise, and we rode off together beautifully – much to the dismay of my buddy. One of my best days ever and of course making me a lifetime believer in Monty's teachings.

Monty Using Mouse's Back as a Podium.
Photo courtesy of Joe Camp.

CHAPTER 11:
TAKE THE TRUST-BASED LEADERSHIP PROFILE

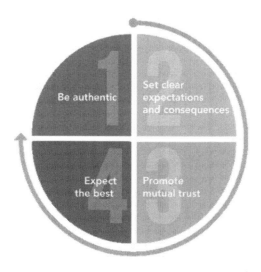

"As a child I watched my father apply the principle, "You do what I tell you to, or I'll hurt you!" to the horses that went through his hands. He often applied the same concept to me. Did the horses feel the same resentment that I did toward the needless pain inflicted upon them? I do not recall learning anything through being physically punished except how to avoid such an incident. Even then, I questioned whether an environment dominated by pain, and therefore fear, was productive. I obeyed him because that was what my father wanted. I loved my horses and knew that I wanted good relationships with them, surmising that there might be a better way.

I was, therefore, from a very early age looking for a way to build a trusting relationship, a 50–50 partnership. Through my observation of the mustangs in the desert and being constantly around horses, it occurred to me, as I watched them moving about in a close-knit herd united for survival, that trust and communication were the keys to their success as a species. After much observation, I could put the rudiments of their language together. I believed that if the horse could trust me, then the whole learning process would speed up. I felt strongly that the answer was through communication. It was many years before I could share my methods with the public. I produced good horses and no one knew how. After my father died, I went public. The rest is history."

- **Monty Roberts,** *The Man Who Listens to Horses*

About the Trust-Based Leadership Profile

Now that you are familiar with the Trust-Based Leadership Model, think about how you show up to others in your own life and work. We have created a self-assessment to help you gauge your development in this area.

This self-assessment is designed to help you think about your own strengths and challenges as you go to create more trust with others. The assessment is a useful way to think about how to improve in some areas, and how to leverage your skills in others.

Take a minute to walk through the exercise and think about the situations you encounter in your work or life. Then tally your results and think about creating an action plan.

Trust-Based Leadership Practices Survey

1 = Never   2 = Seldom
3 = Sometimes 4 = Often
5 = Always

Question	1	2	3	4	5
1. To what extent do you engage others through personal sincerity?					
2. To what extent do you reinforce others' sense of self-worth?					
3. To what extent do you set clear and fair expectations before a work request?					
4. To what extent do you clarify consequences in a fair and timely way?					
5. To what extent do you try to avoid intimidation in your relationship with others?					
6. To what extent do you attempt to build and repair trust through open dialogue and communication?					
7. To what extent do you express performance goals in compelling and engaging ways?					
8. To what extent do you offer meaningful challenges to encourage personal motivation?					

Are you a trust-worthy leader? How easily do you trust others? The TBLP is an assessment that captures the four leadership practices of a trust-based leader, and is from the book, ***Horse Sense for Leaders: Developing Trust-Based Relationships.***

Review the items below and place an "X" in the area that best represents your true tendencies within that area:

How to score your survey:

Review the location of the X's you placed on the above survey. Place the numeric score of each X next to the question line on the score sheet below. Then, add the question scores and place a total in the total box.

Interpreting your scores-Your Trust Quotient

Your **Trust Quotient** is the sum of your responses within each practice area. Notice where your total scores fall. What scores indicate areas of strength? What scores indicate a need to challenge yourself and work toward improvement?

Scoring   Total

Question 1 _____ + Question 2 _____ = [   ] be authentic.
Question 3 _____ + Question 4 _____ = [   ] set clear expectations & consequences.
Question 5 _____ + Question 6 _____ = [   ] promote mutual trust.
Question 7 _____ + Question 8 _____ = [   ] expect the best.

Developed by Stephanie Tribo, The Corporate Learning Institute, 2015

Trust-Based Leadership Action Planner

Your profile provides a personalized learning process to help you leverage your strengths, challenges, and to learn to work with others more effectively. To focus on how you can use your results at work, answer the questions below:

What area of Trust-Based Leadership did you score highest on?

How can you begin to leverage your strengths by using them more effectively at work?

What area of Trust-Based Leadership did you score lowest on?

To improve in these areas, think about using information detailed on the following page and choose
the best approach for you. What steps can you take to improve your lowest score?

Step 4: Read the Tips for Building Trust as a Leader

Your TBLP results gives you a quick insight into you as a leader by measuring you on each of the four Trust-Based Leadership Practices. How well do others trust you and how well do you trust others?

While the four steps of the model are often related, your scores may be higher in some areas than others. This assessment shows which areas you are strongest in, and which areas you might want to improve in order to be a more trust-based leader.

Trust-Based Practice: Tips for Developing Yourself in This Area:

1. Be authentic.	<ul><li>Be yourself; know, acknowledge, and value your uniqueness and many facets.</li><li>Offer sincerity over pretention.</li><li>Acknowledge other's value and worth by not attacking who they are.</li></ul>
2. Set clear Expectations And consequence.	<ul><li>Be prepared to give clear expectations upfront.</li><li>If possible, state your wants and needs and ask for input from others.</li><li>Clarify any consequences that may happen upfront.</li></ul>
4. Promote mutual trust.	<ul><li>Offer honesty and be careful about being too blunt.</li><li>Modify your interactions to move from judging to seeking understanding.</li><li>Repair trust by risking vulnerability and sincerely reaching out.</li></ul>
4. Expect the best.	<ul><li>Clearly articulate goals in interesting and compelling ways.</li><li>Create enriched opportunities at work to fully engage others.</li><li>Know that failure is the cousin of success; re-label "failure" as "learning."</li></ul>

Other Ideas for Developing Trust

- ✓ Research supports that getting to know each other at work on a deeper level helps people collaborate better.

- ✓ Think about rearranging the office or offering more opportunities for informal contact.

- ✓ Provide training in managing conflict.

- ✓ Create group norms or shared expectations that support honesty, caring and a mutual commitment to results.

Buy the book, Horse Sense for Leaders; Building Trust-Based Relationships here.

CLI provides coaching, training, and strategic planning services to help your business grow. Contact us at corplearning@corplearning.com or at 800.203.6734.

AFTERWORD

"If all learning is 1-10, then the most important part of learning is 0-1. If a horse or a person is about to learn, stay out of their way.

My system is to watch for the horse or human to do something right and to congratulate them for it without pain or restraint. When learning, I always say; 'Adrenalin up, learning down. Adrenalin down, learning up.'

In my own life, my greatest accomplishment was learning to be gentle. Without that, I would have accomplished nothing. Horses, and humans need patience. If you act like you have only 15 minutes, it will take all day. Act like you've got all day and it will only take 15 minutes.

The major source of satisfaction that I have received from working with horses and humans in this way is the verification by both of what my work means to them."

-Monty Roberts

We hope this book inspires you to learn from the leadership experts; horses. Even more, we challenge you to dig in and apply some of Monty's discoveries to your own life.

A MONTY ROBERTS TUTORIAL

About Join-Up®
Monty Roberts first developed **Join-Up®** to stop the cycle of violence typically used in traditional horse breaking. Through a process of clear communication and mutual trust, horses are motivated to be willing partners as they accept the first saddle, bridle, and rider of their lives in less than thirty minutes.

Watch a Join-Up® Here:
https://www.youtube.com/watch?v=9Dx91mH2voo

An interesting conversation with Monty and British actor Martin Clunes

Martin Clunes is one of England's most-loved actors. Martin and Monty share their passion for horses in this interesting conversation.

Watch Monty and Martin Clunes:
https://www.youtube.com/watch?v=CgcoCAwylW4
Watch Monty and Martin Clunes complete a Join-Up®:
https://www.youtube.com/watch?v=0jATGwEaIvs

Learn About Shy Boy: The Mustang Who Came In From The Wild
Shy Boy is the Mustang that Monty adopted and who still lives at Flag Is Up Farms.

Watch Monty and Shy Boy:
https://www.youtube.com/watch?v=4BB4XCdQCts

ABOUT THE AUTHORS

Susan Cain, Ed.D., LCSW, is a business consultant and coach, mother and life-long equestrian. She is a partner with Dr. Tim Buividas at the Corporate Learning Institute, an established consultancy based in Chicago, Illinois. She serves as adjunct faculty at several Chicago area business schools. Susan's practice includes an international base of clientele. The Corporate Learning Institute provides custom-designed training solutions, strategic planning and performance coaching solutions. Learn more about Susan at https://www.linkedin.com/pub/dr-susan-cain/2/8bb/b02

Debbie Roberts-Loucks joined MPRI in 2002 to build Monty Roberts' international training schedule and oversee MPRI's publishing, product development, and licensing. A graduate of UCLA, Debbie has extensive experience in sales, marketing, and new business development. Debbie's extensive background with horses, as well as her commitment to advance Monty's concepts, uniquely qualifies her to extend the MPRI brand into a global leadership organization impacting millions of individuals, companies, organizations, governments, and industries. Learn more about Debbie at http://www.linkedin.com/in/debbieloucks.

ADDITIONAL RESOURCES AND WEBSITES

Block, Peter. Community; the Structure of Belonging. Berrett-Koehler Publishers, 2009.

Brown, Brene. Daring Greatly: How the Courage to Be Vulnerable Transforms the Way We Live, Love, Parent, and Lead. Gotham, 2012.

Cain, Susan and Roberts-Loucks, Debbie. Life Lessons From The Man Who Listens to Horses, 2012.

Clifton, D.O., & Hodges, T.D. (in press). Strengths. In J.M. Burns (Ed.), The Encyclopedia of Leadership. Thousand Oaks, CA: Sage.

Haller, Howard Edward. Adversity and Obstacles in the Shaping of prominent leaders; A Hermeneutic Phenomenological Inquiry. The Leadership Success Institute and Gonzaga University Doctoral Dissertation in Leadership Studies, 2008.

Haque, Umami. The New Capitalist Manifesto: Building a Disruptively Better Business. Harvard Business Review Press, 2010.

Pink, Dan. Drive: The Surprising Truth about What Motivates Us. Riverhead Books, 2011.

Rath, Tom. How Full is Your Bucket? Positive Strategies for Work and Life. Gallup Press, 2004.

Roberts, Monty. The Man who Listens to Horses, The Story of a Real-Life Horse Whisperer. Random House Digital, 2008.

Scott, Susan. Fierce Conversations: Achieving Success at Work and in Life One Conversation at a Time. Berkeley Trade, 2004.

Websites Accessed:

www.corplearning.com
www.clisresroucecenter.com
www.amazon.com/Susan-Cain/e/B00AVZINSU
www.montyroberts.com
www.facebook.com/LifeLessonsFromTheManWhoListensToHorses
www.facebook.com/montyrobertsworkshop?ref=h

OTHER BOOKS BY MONTY ROBERTS

Roberts, Monty. The Man Who Listens to Horses. Random House, August 1997, hardcover, 310 pages. ISBN 0-345-42705-X.

Roberts, Monty. The Man Who Listens to Horses - abridged audio book. Random House Audio, August 1997. ISBN 978-0-679-46044-2.

Roberts, Monty. Shy Boy, the Horse that Came in from the Wild. 1999, 239 pages. ISBN 0-676-97273-X.

Roberts, Monty. Horse Sense for People: The Man Who Listens to Horses Talks to People. 2002, 256 pages. ISBN 0-670-89975-5.

Roberts, Monty. From My Hands to Yours: Lessons from a Lifetime of Training Championship Horses. 2002, 230 pages. ISBN 192925656.

Roberts, Monty. The Horses in My Life. 2002, 256 pages. ISBN 0755313453.

Roberts, Monty. Ask Monty: Over 170 Most Common Horse Problems Solved. 2009, 320 pages. ISBN 0755317238.

Roberts, Monty. I'm Shy Boy: Here's My Story. Solvang, CA: M. and P. Roberts, 2010. Print. ISBN 978-1-929256-61-7.

Roberts, Monty. The Little American Mustang. Solvang, CA: Monty and Pat Roberts, 2010. Print.

IMAGE CREDITS

Special thanks to Afonso Westphal and Bob Viering.

You can reach Afonso Westphal at afonso@mundoequestre.com.br and Bob Viering at bob@riverpointusa.com.

APPENDIX

Discussion and Leadership Questions by Chapter:

Chapter 1: A Transformational Leadership Story: Monty Manages Change, Encounters Resistance, and Overcomes Setbacks in Brazil

Leadership Questions to consider:

• Have you worked in an environment with hierarchical leadership and top-down command? How did this affect your job performance? What was negative/positive about it?

• How strong is your personal ability to inspire others as a leader (transformational leadership)?

• Which of the four components of transformational leadership resonate most with you? Which of those four are most important for you to have in your boss in order to help you succeed at work?

• How do you handle resistance when it appears as an obstacle to reach your goals?

Chapter 2: The Four Practices of the Trust-Based Leadership Practices Model

Leadership Questions to consider:

• How does trust form the basis of Monty's empire?

• What core message are people drawn to?

• How can this inform my own assumptions about how I am leading others?

• Which of the four components of Monty's trust based leadership model (be authentic, set expectations, promote mutual trust, expect the best) do you embody the most? Which one do you struggle maintaining?

• Knowing that man is a "fight" animal, how do associated traits of preoccupation with the chase and having dominance show up in your work style and in your personal life?

Chapter 3: The Need for Trust-Based Leadership in an Unpredictable World

Leadership Questions to consider:

• What role does trust play in managing inter-generational differences?

• How does Monty encourage his young staff to excel?

• Do you see the value in humility as a leadership quality? Why do you think that some leaders struggle to embody it?

• Monty points out that some leaders focus on the wrong issues and instead are overly concerned with personal appearances and popularity; how might this show up in a work environment? What is the last impact of a leader who does this?

• Integrity is intertwined with the idea of perspective, being able to see both sides of situation; why can taking perspective become challenging at work?

Chapter 4: Towards a Deeper Definition of Trust

Leadership Questions to Consider:

• What is your own working model for developing trust with people who work for or with you?

• How can you balance the forces of mutual trust with high expectations?

• What optimal approach can you take to repairing trust?

• Do you feel that trust is worth the risk?

• What are your personal experiences with trust in your work relationships/ how might that effect your ability to trust others in a work setting?

• Do you believe than innovation and creativity thrive when you don't have to ask for permission? Why or why not?

Chapter 5: The Four Trust-Based Leadership Practice

Leadership Questions to Consider:

• How do you define authentic leadership for yourself?

• How can you show others personal sincerity in the workplace?

• Can you think of a time when a leader reinforced your sense of self-worth? Why is this important in a corporate environment?

• Given what you've learned about qualities of successful leaders, what is your vision of the "ideal" leader?

• What is your reaction to the idea of authenticity in leader? Do you think it is possible to show up to work every day and truly be authentic?

• What do you think will be your biggest obstacles in becoming a more authentic leader?

Chapter 6: The Four Trust-Based Leadership Practices: Setting Clear Expectations and Consequences

Leadership Questions to Consider:

• What are some ways that communication has become convoluted in your workplace?

• Which of the 7 deadly sins of making demands do you resonate with most?

• Can you describe a situation where a communication problem occurred because it was done using technology and not in person?

• How could this have gone differently?

Chapter 7: The Four Trust-Based Leadership Practices: Promote Mutual Trust

Leadership questions to consider:

• How does this affect your thinking about those at work who need extra patience?

• How would it affect that relationship for you to apply these concepts?

• How could you apply some of the principles of accelerated readiness as exemplified through the motivational interviewing process?

• Do you believe that trust is a capacity and not an emotion; the capacity of one person to let go of control and turn it over to another?

• What will it take for you trust others more at your workplace?

Chapter 8: The Four Trust-Based Leadership Practices: Expect the Best From Others

Leadership questions to consider:

• Do you feel your current workplace gives you the autonomy you need to master complex tasks? If not, how can you communicate your needs to change this?

• What does author, Dan Pink, state are the 3 main motivators that drive individuals to perform at their best?

• Do you think it is possible for leaders to make projects and goals more meaningful for followers to ensure success? Why or why not?

Chapter 9: Follow-Up - Ensuring Long-Term Performance Gains

Leadership questions to consider:

• Monty notes the importance of communicating clear next steps and expectations; What is a problem you notice in regards to communicating clean expectations at your work environment?

• What is the most effective method to remove assumptions in communication?

Chapter 10: An Action Plan - Applying Trust-Based Leadership in Your Life and Work

Leadership considerations:

• Consider putting timelines on your action plan.

• Consider sharing your action plan with others to increase your motivation and personal accountability.

REFERENCES

References Chapter 1

Bass B, Riggio R. *Transformational Leadership* (2Nd Ed.) [e-book]. Mahwah, NJ, US: Lawrence Erlbaum Associates Publishers; 2006. Available from: PsycINFO, Ipswich, MA.

References Chapter 2

Covey, S., & Merrill, R. (2006). *The speed of trust: The one thing that changes everything.* New York: Free Press.

Stephenson, Karen (2005). *Quantum Theory of Trust: The Secret of Mapping and Managing Human Relationships* ("Financial Times") Hardcover

References Chapter 3

2012 *Global Workforce Study.* (2012, July 1). Retrieved August 29, 2014, from http://www.towerswatson.com/Insights/IC-Types/Survey-Research-Results/2012/07/2012-Towers-Watson-Global-Workforce-Study

15th Annual Global CEO Survey. (2012, January 21). Retrieved August 29, 2014, from http://www.pwc.com/gx/en/ceo-survey/2012/index.jhtml

Toossi, M. (2005, November 1). *Labor force projections to 2014: Retiring boomers.* Retrieved August 29, 2014

References Chapter 4

Bidault, F., & Castello, A. (2010*). Trust and creativity: Understanding the *role of trust in creativity-oriented joint developments.* R&D Management, 259-270

Galbraith, J. (2009). *Designing Matrix Organizations That Actually Work: How IBM, Procter & Gamble, And Others Design For Success* By Jay R. Galbraith. Personnel Psychology, 639-642.

Gibb, J. R., & Robertson, V. M. (1978). *Trust: A new view of personal and organizational development.* Los Angeles: Guild of Tutors Press

Johnson, S. (2010). *Where good ideas come from: The natural history of innovation.* New York: Riverhead Books.

Mayer, R. C., Davis, J. H., & Schoorman, F. D. (1995). *An Integrative Model of Organizational Trust.* Academy of Management Review, 20, 709–734.

McGregor, D. (1967). *The Professional Manager.* New York: McGraw-Hill.

Morieux, Y., & Tollman, P. (2014). Six Simple Rules: How to Manage Complexity Without Getting Complicated.

Rousseau, D. M., Sitkin, S. B., Burt, R. S., & Camerer, C. (1998). *"Not So Different After All: A Cross-Discipline View of Trust."* Academy of Management Review, 23, 393–404.

Zalta, E. (2013, January 1). S*tanford Encyclopedia of Philosophy.* Retrieved September 2, 2014, from http://plato.stanford.edu/search/searcher.py?query=trust definition.

References Chapter 5

Avolio, B. J., Gardner, W. L., Walumbwa, F. O., Luthans, F., & May, D. R. (2004*). "Unlocking The Mask: A Look At The Process By Which Authentic Leaders Impact Follower Attitudes and Behaviors."* The

Leadership Quarterly, 15, 801–823.

Blau, P. M. 1964. *Exchange and Power in Social Life*. New York: John Wiley.

Brown, Brene (2010-09-20). *The Gifts of Imperfection: Let Go of Who You Think You're Supposed to Be and Embrace Who You Are* (p. 50). Hazelden Publishing. Kindle Edition.

Dirks, K. T. & Ferrin, D. L. (2002*).* *"Trust in Leadership: Meta-Analytic Findings and Implications for Organizational Research."* Journal of Applied Psychology, 87, 611-628.

George, B., Sims, P., McLean, A., & Mayer, D. (2007, February 1). *"Discovering Your Authentic Leadership."* Retrieved September 2, 2014, from http://hbr.org/2007/02/discovering-your-authentic-leadership/ar/1

Jung, D. I., & Avolio, B. J. (2000). *"Opening the Black Box: An Experimental Investigation of the Mediating Effects of Trust and Value Congruence on Transformational and Transactional Leadership."* Journal of Organizational Behavior, 21, 949–964.

Konovsky, M.A. & Pugh, S.D. (1994). *"Citizenship Behaviour and Social Exchange."* Academy of Management Journal, 37 (3), 656- 669.

Mayer, R. C., Davis, J. H., & Schoorman, F. D. (1995). *"An Integrative Model of Organizational Trust."* Academy of Management Review, 20, 709 –734.

References Chapter 6

12 Tips to Reduce Employee Turnover | Globoforce Blog. (2013, October 1). Retrieved December 22, 2014, from http://www.globoforce.com/gfblog/2013/12-surefire-tips-to-reduce-employee-turnover/

Ashkenas, R. (2010). *Simply Effective: How to Cut Through Complexity in Your Organization and Get Things Done.* Boston, Mass.: Harvard Business Press.

Batz, J. (2013). *Improving the Performance Review Process.* Biz Library.

Fain, S. (2014, September 2). *Bullet to head – Moneyball.* [Video file]. Retrieved from https://www.youtube.com/watch?v=jXEtOPMW2hM

Kaput, M. (2013). *Account Managers: Advice for Giving and Receiving Constructive Feedback.* Market Agency Insider.

Thorne, E. (2013). *Recognition to the Rescue.* Achievers.

Rubin, I. M., Plovnick, M. S., & Fry, R. E. (1977). *Task-Oriented Team Development.* New York: McGraw-Hill.

Stone, D., & Heen, S. (2013). *Thanks for the Feedback: The Science and Art of Receiving Feedback Well (Even When it is Off Base, Unfair, Poorly Delivered, and Frankly, You're Not in the Mood).*

References Chapter 7

Camp, J. (2011). *Why Relationship First Works: Why and How it Changes Everything.* United States: 14 Hands Press.

Knerr, Robert. (1987). *Bacstop Manual.* Pretty Lake Adventure Center.

Miller, W. R., & Rollnick, S. (2012). *Motivational interviewing: Helping people change* (3rd ed.). New York: Guilford Press.

Stephenson, Karen (2005). *Quantum Theory of Trust: The Secret of Mapping and Managing Human Relationship*s ("Financial Times") Hardcover.

The Uncanny Valley of a Functional Organization - Stratechery by Ben Thompson. (2013, July 16). Retrieved December 22, 2014, from http://stratechery.com/2013/the-uncanny-valley-of-a-functional-organization/

References Chapter 8

Brophy, Jere. 1986. *On motivating students.* ERIC document ED 276 724. (cited in Lumsden, 1997).

Friedel, R. (2007). *A Culture of Improvement: Technology and the Western Millennium.* Cambridge, Mass.: MIT Press.

Lumsden, Linda. 1997. *Expectations for students.* ERIC document ED 409 609.

Pink, Daniel H. (2009). *Drive: the surprising truth about what motivates us.* New York, NY.

Sterling Livingston, J. (1969). *Pygmalion in Management.* Harvard Business Review Classic.

Vaitheeswar & Carson. (Oct. 11, 2007). *The Age of Mass Innovation.* The Economist. http://www.economist.com/node/9928291

Yukl, G.(1999). *An evaluation of conceptual weaknesses in transformational and charismatic leadership theories.* Leadership Quarterly, 10, 285-305;http://dx.doi.org/10.1016/S1048-9843(99)00013-2Riverhead Books

References Chapter 9

Covey, S. (2009, May 1). *How the Best Leaders Build Trust* by Stephen M. R. Covey @ LeadershipNow. Retrieved December 22, 2014, from http://www.leadershipnow.com/CoveyOnTrust.html

Made in the USA
Las Vegas, NV
13 October 2021